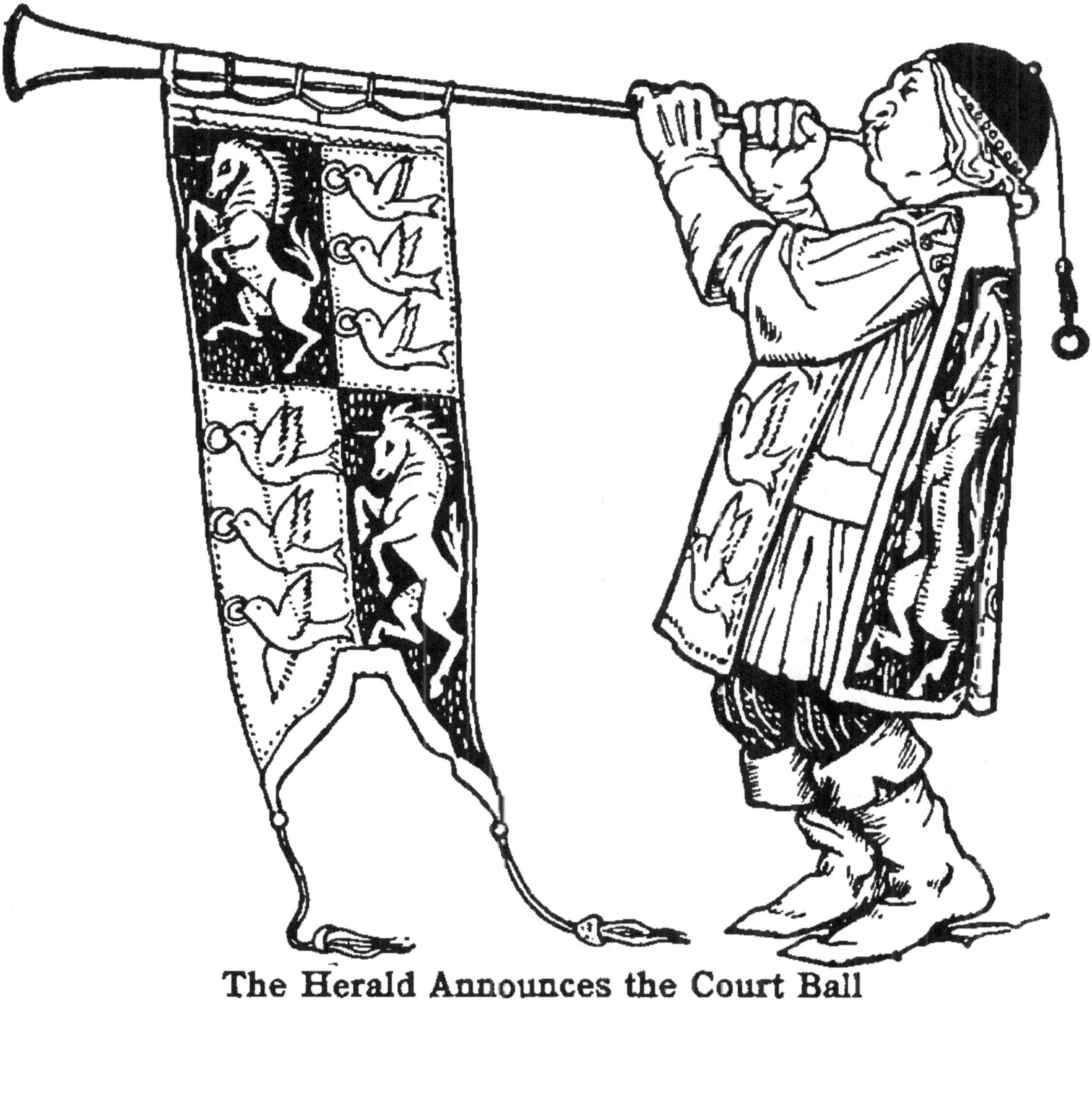

The Herald Announces the Court Ball

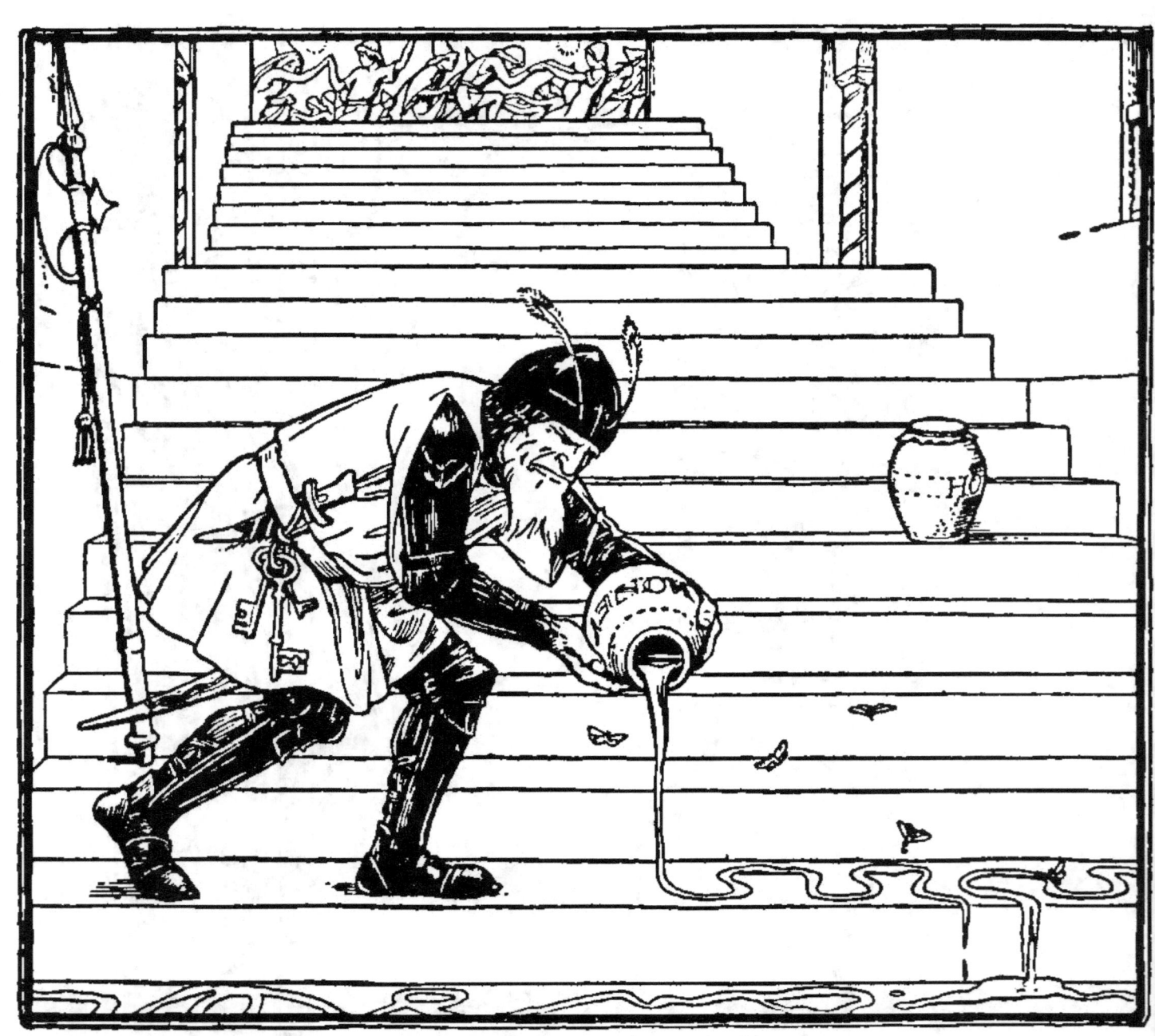

The Soldier Lays a Honey Trap

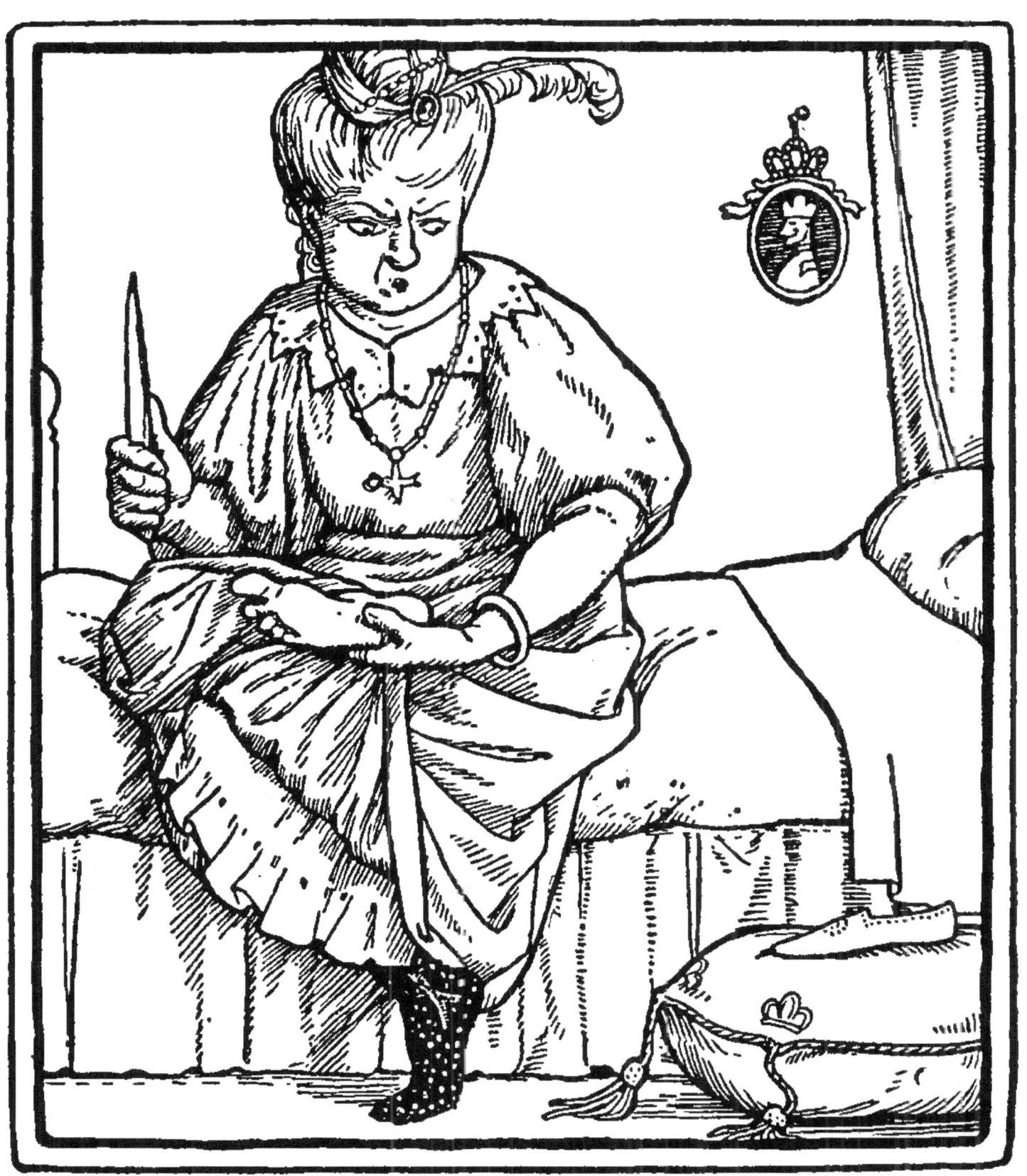

The Step-Sister Cuts off her Toe

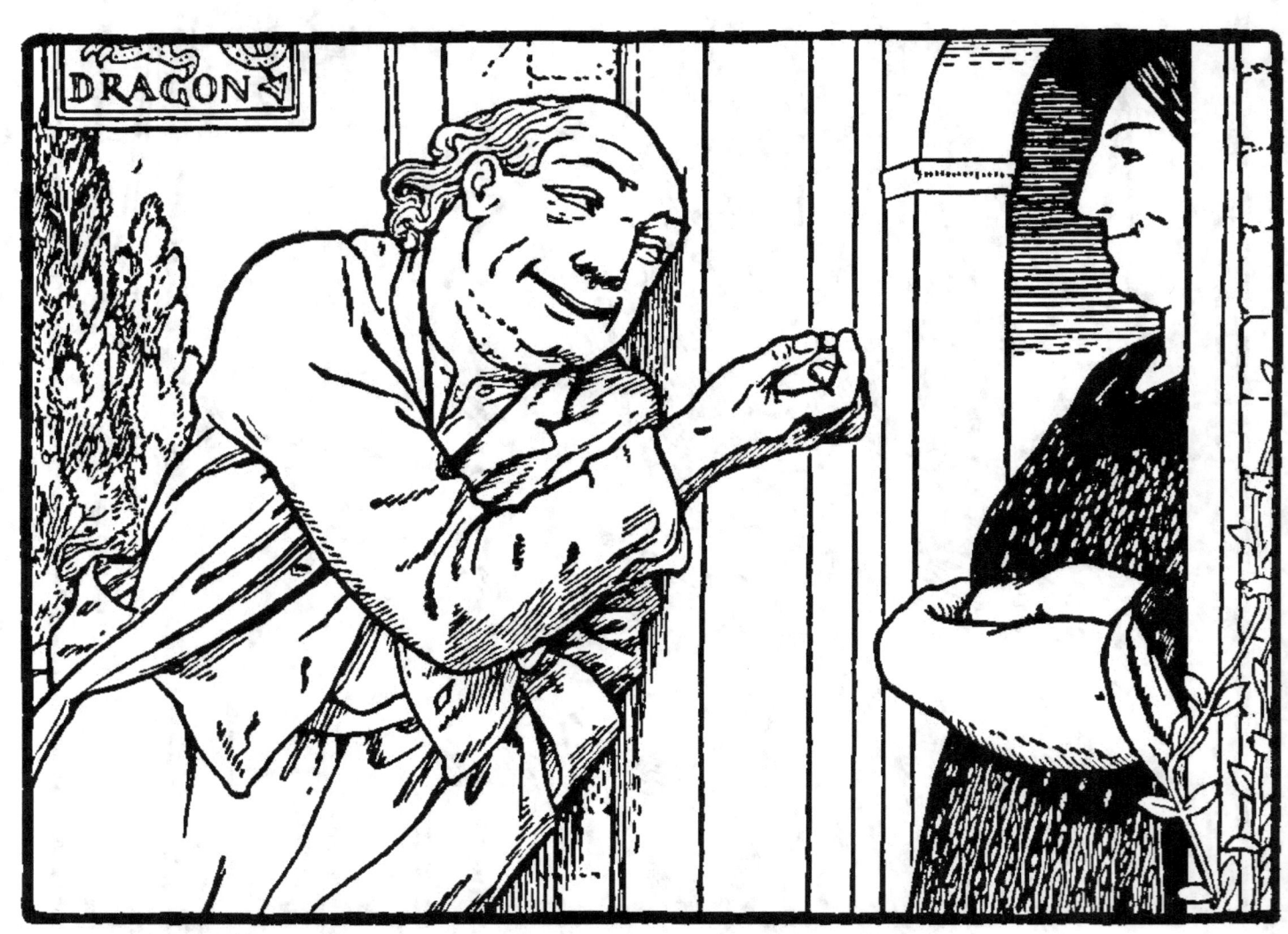

"Will you Mind my Pea?"

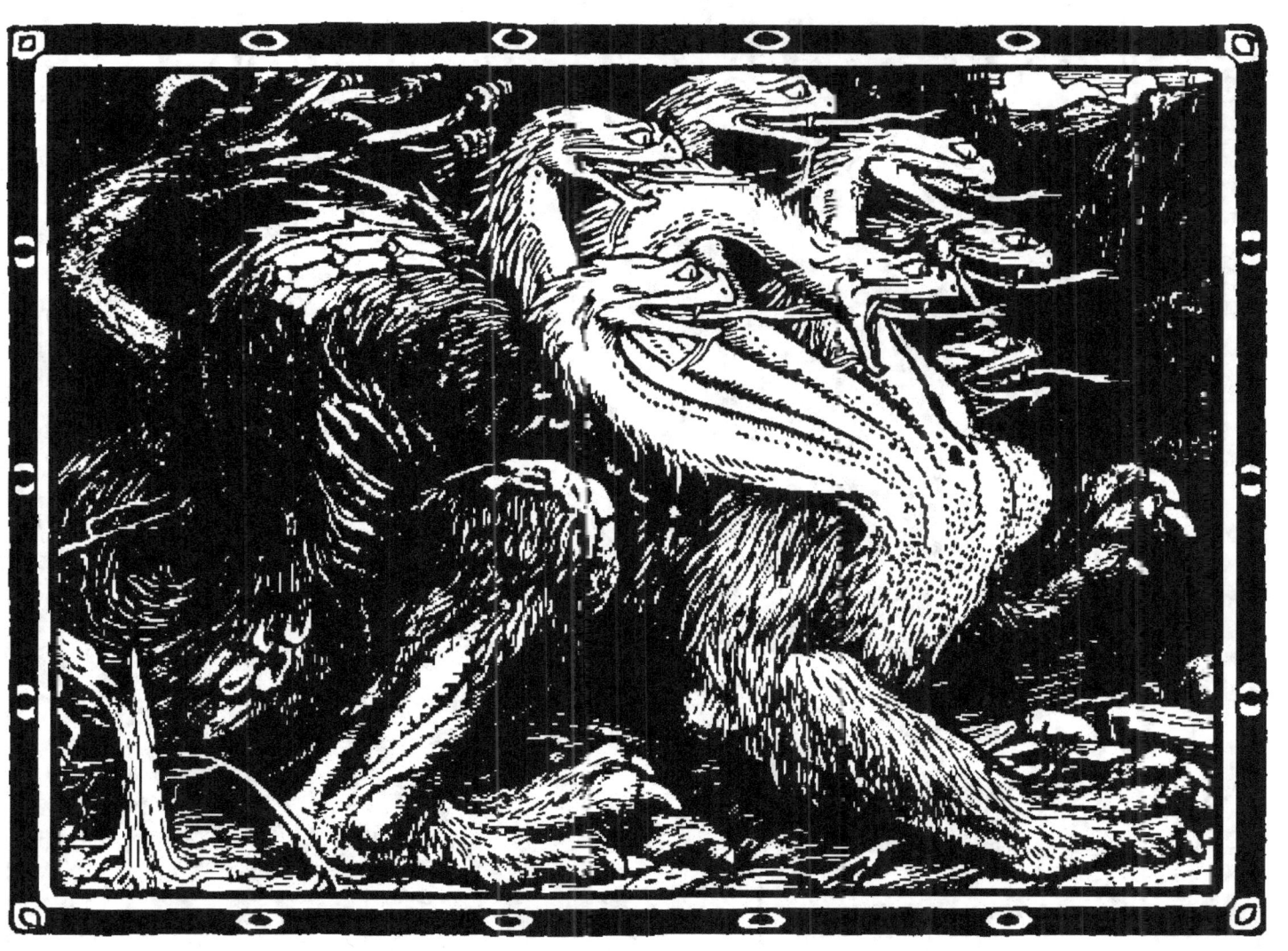

The Seven-Headed Dragon

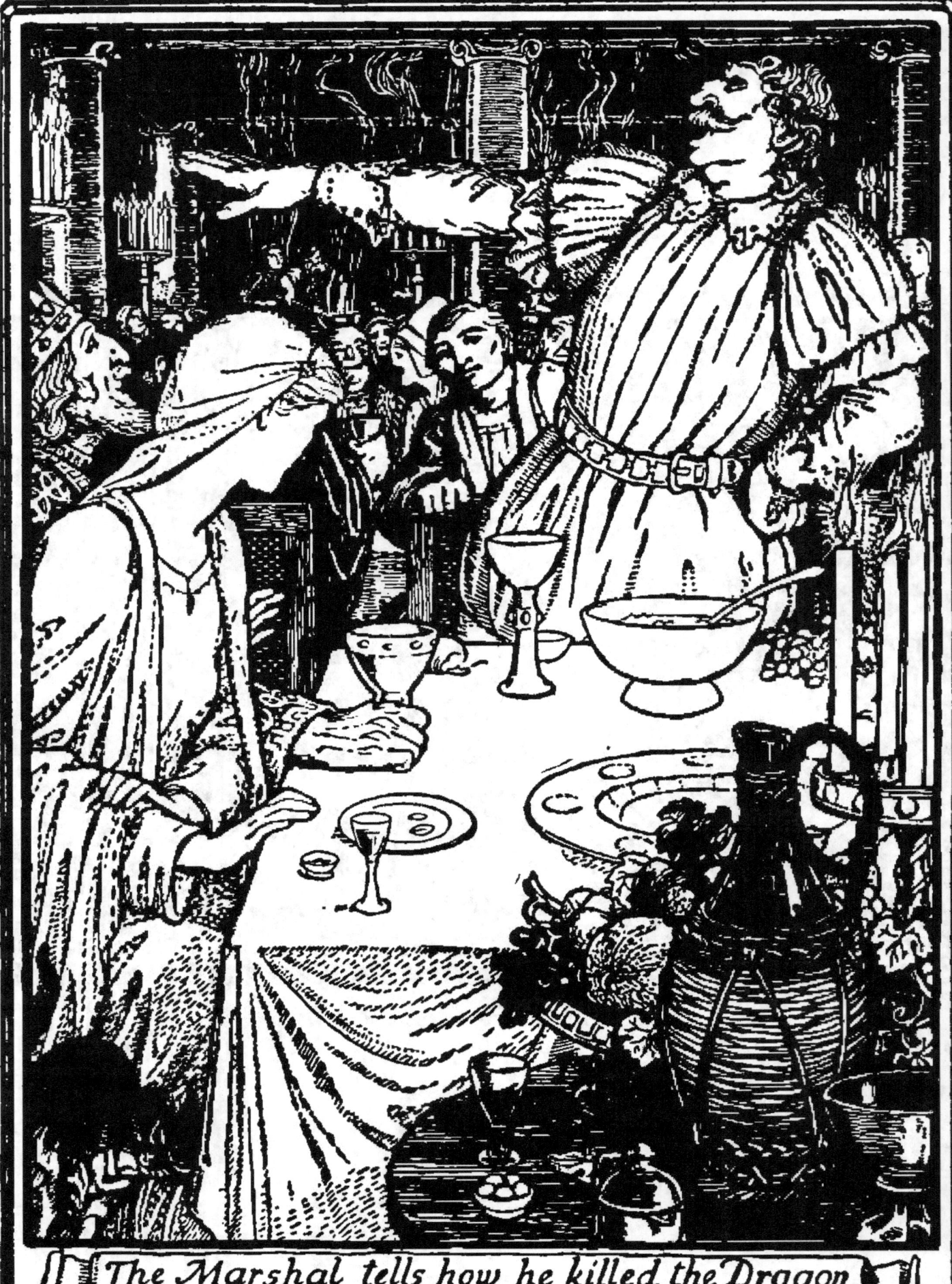
The Marshal tells how he killed the Dragon

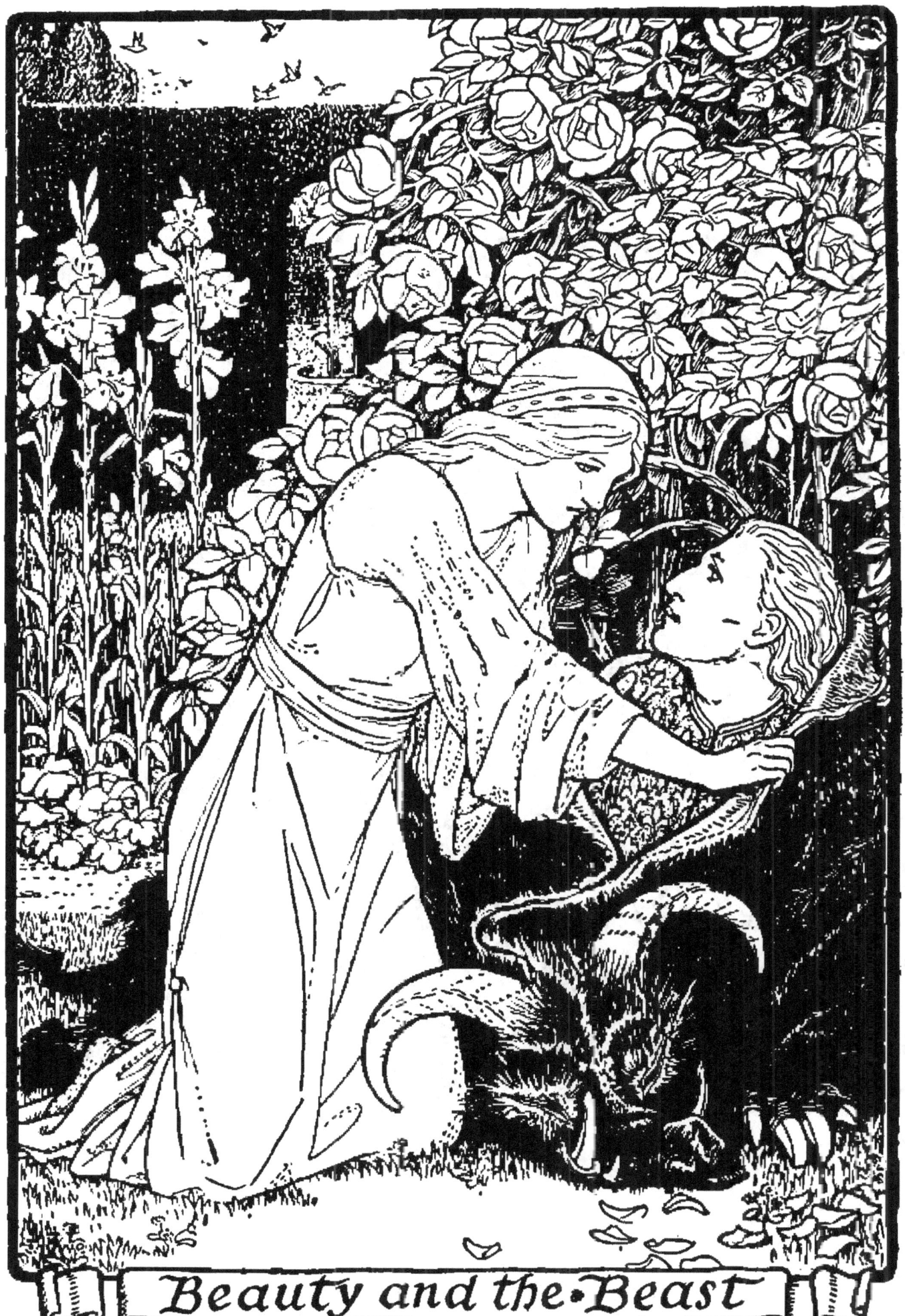
Beauty and the Beast

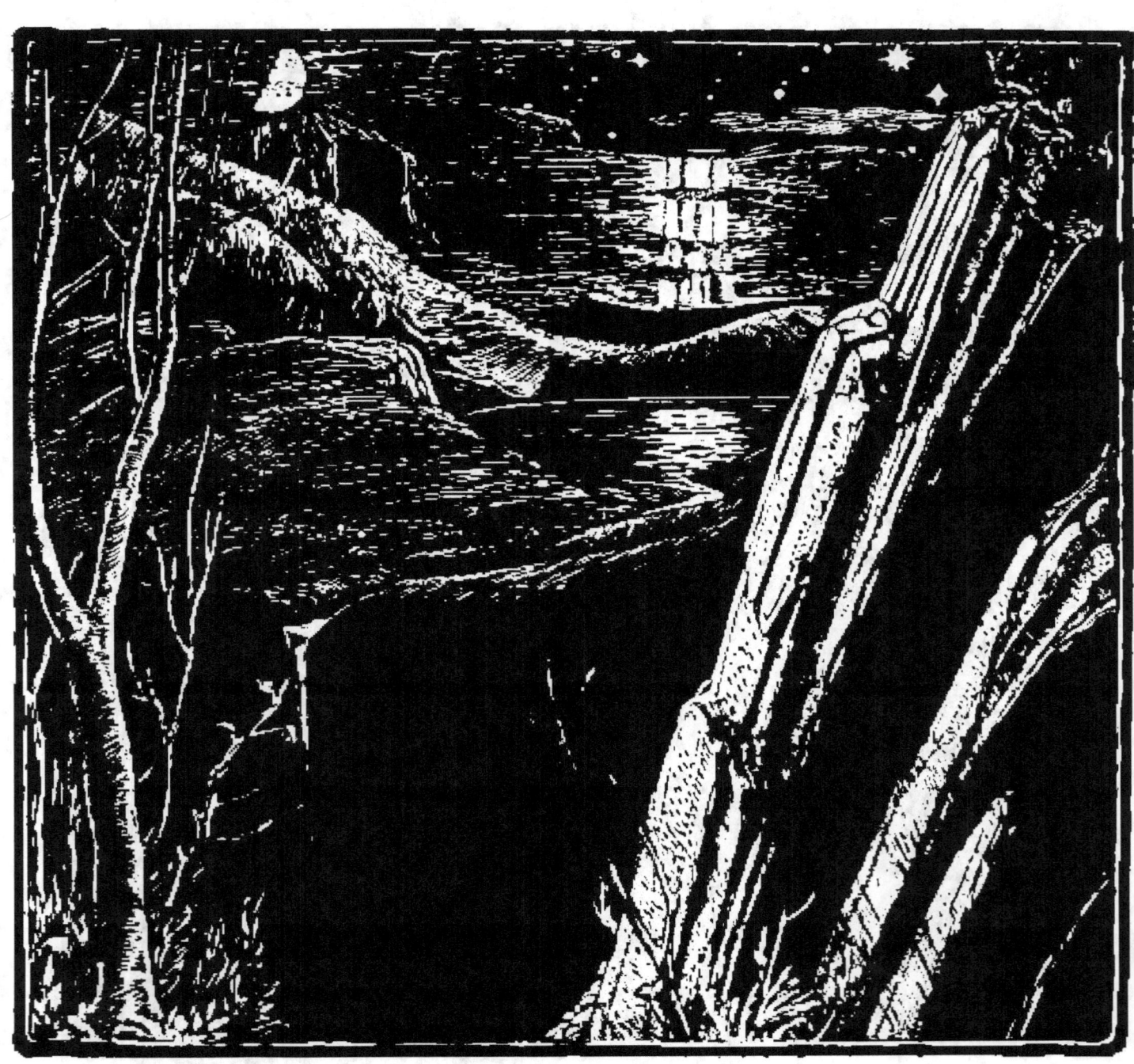

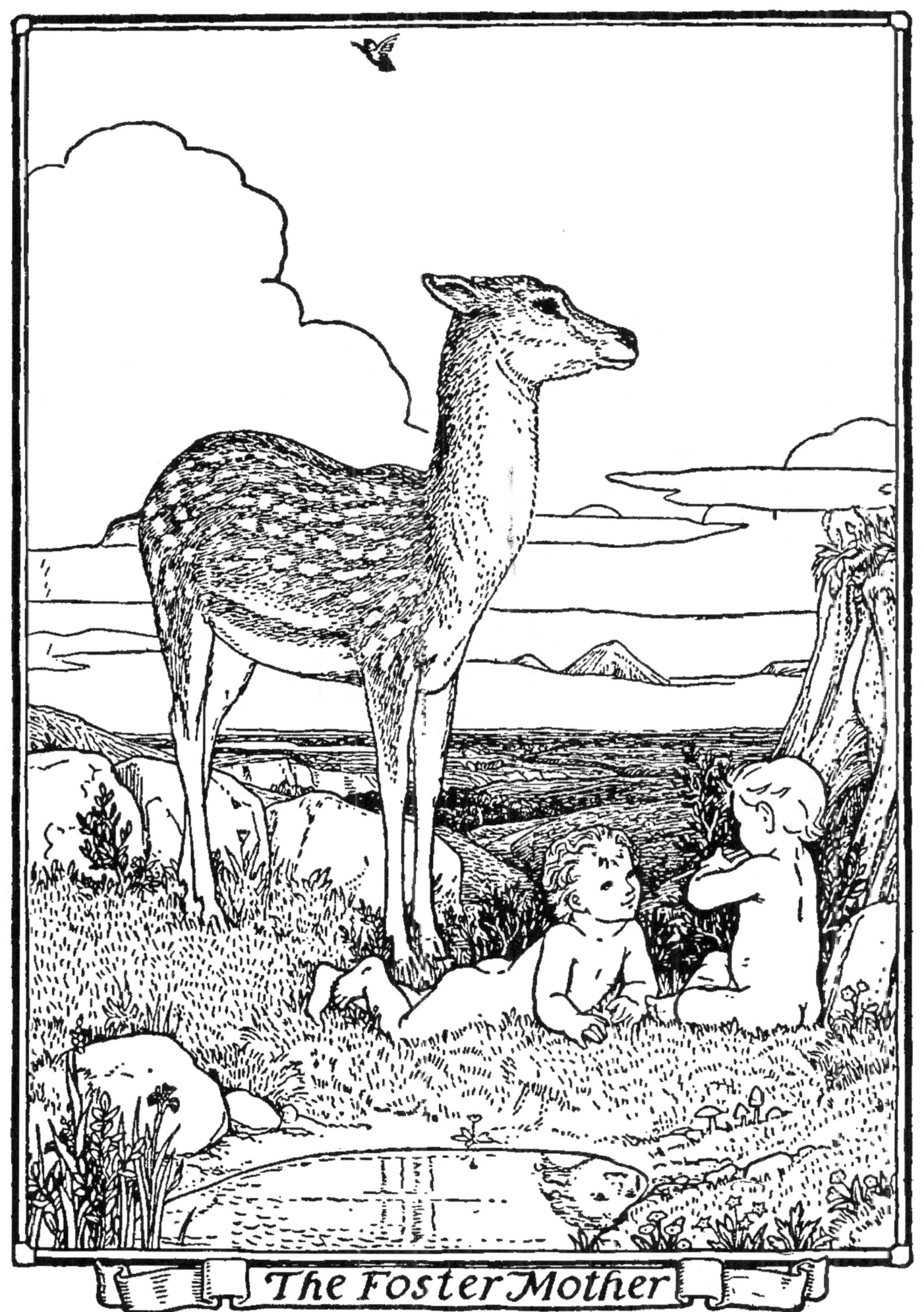

The Foster Mother

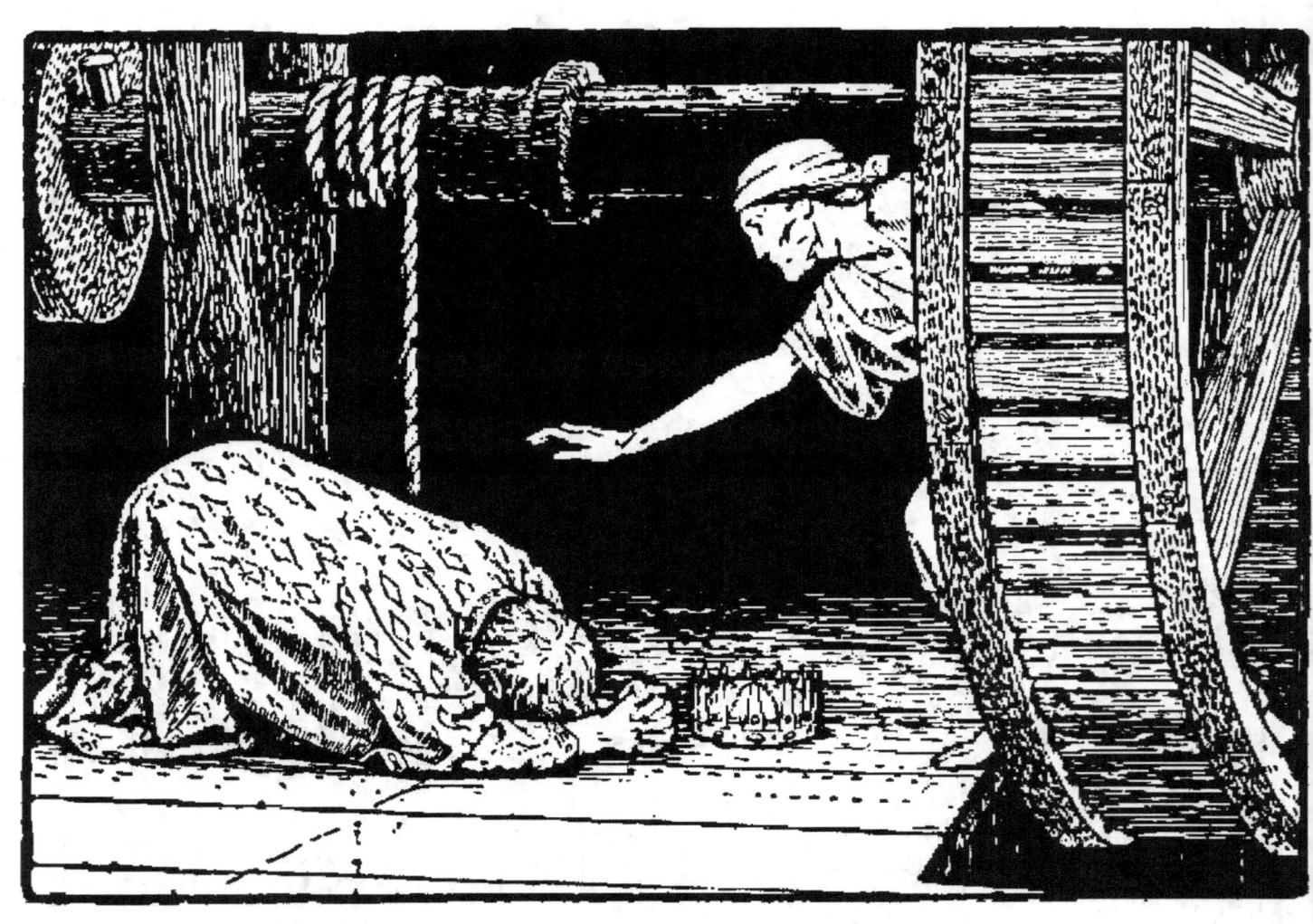

The King Begs Pardon

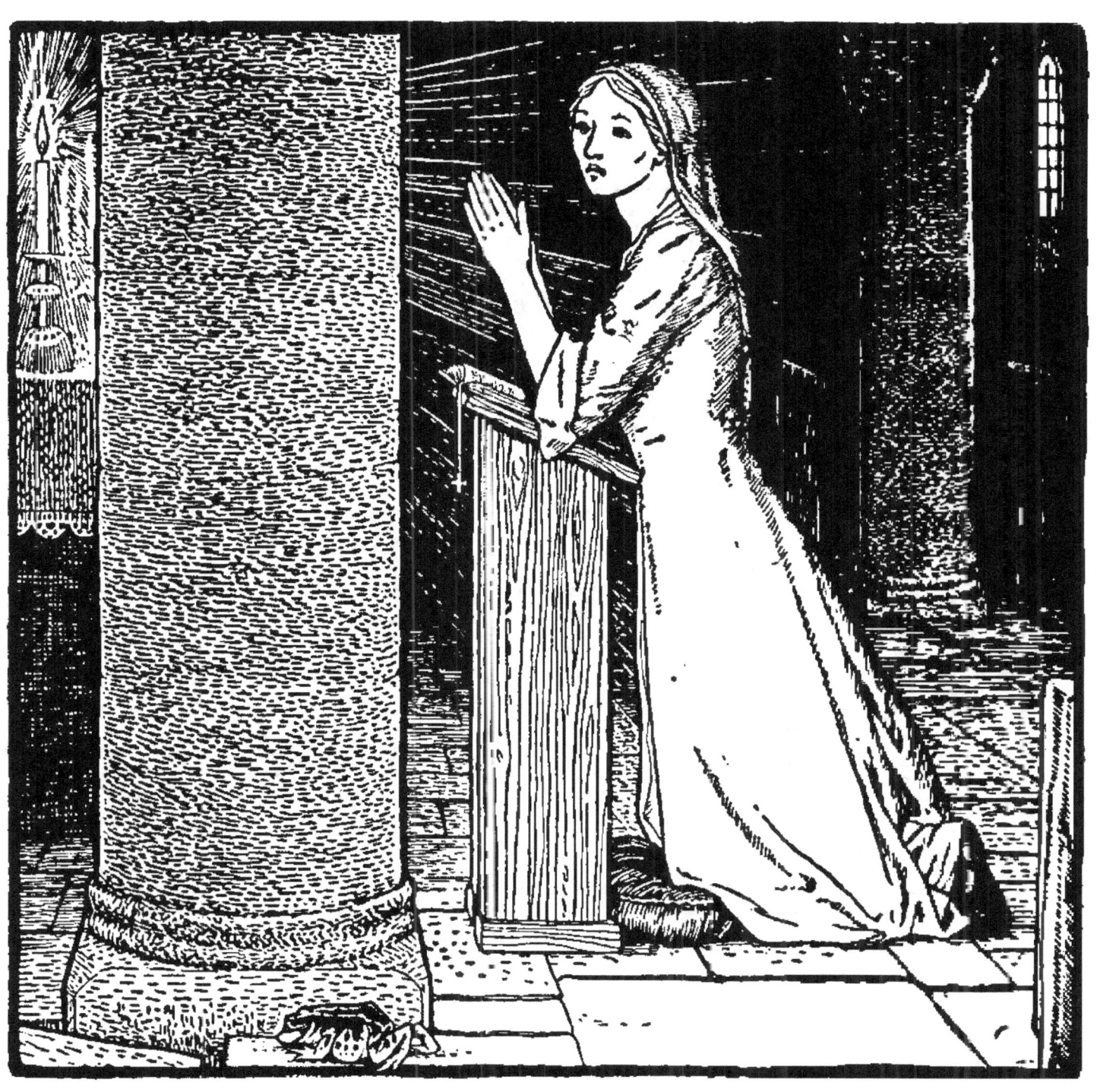

The Girl and the Frog

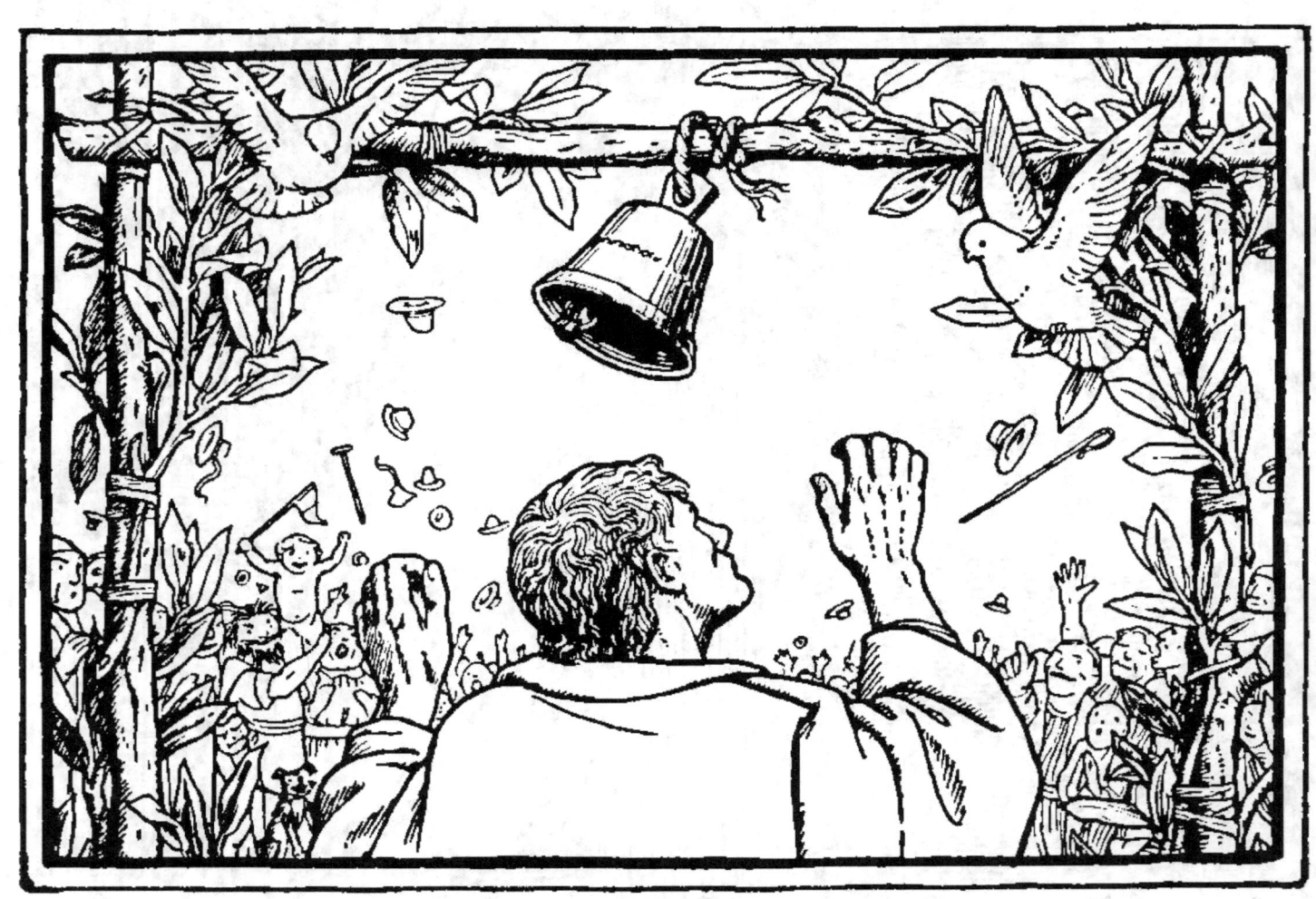

The Pope is Elected

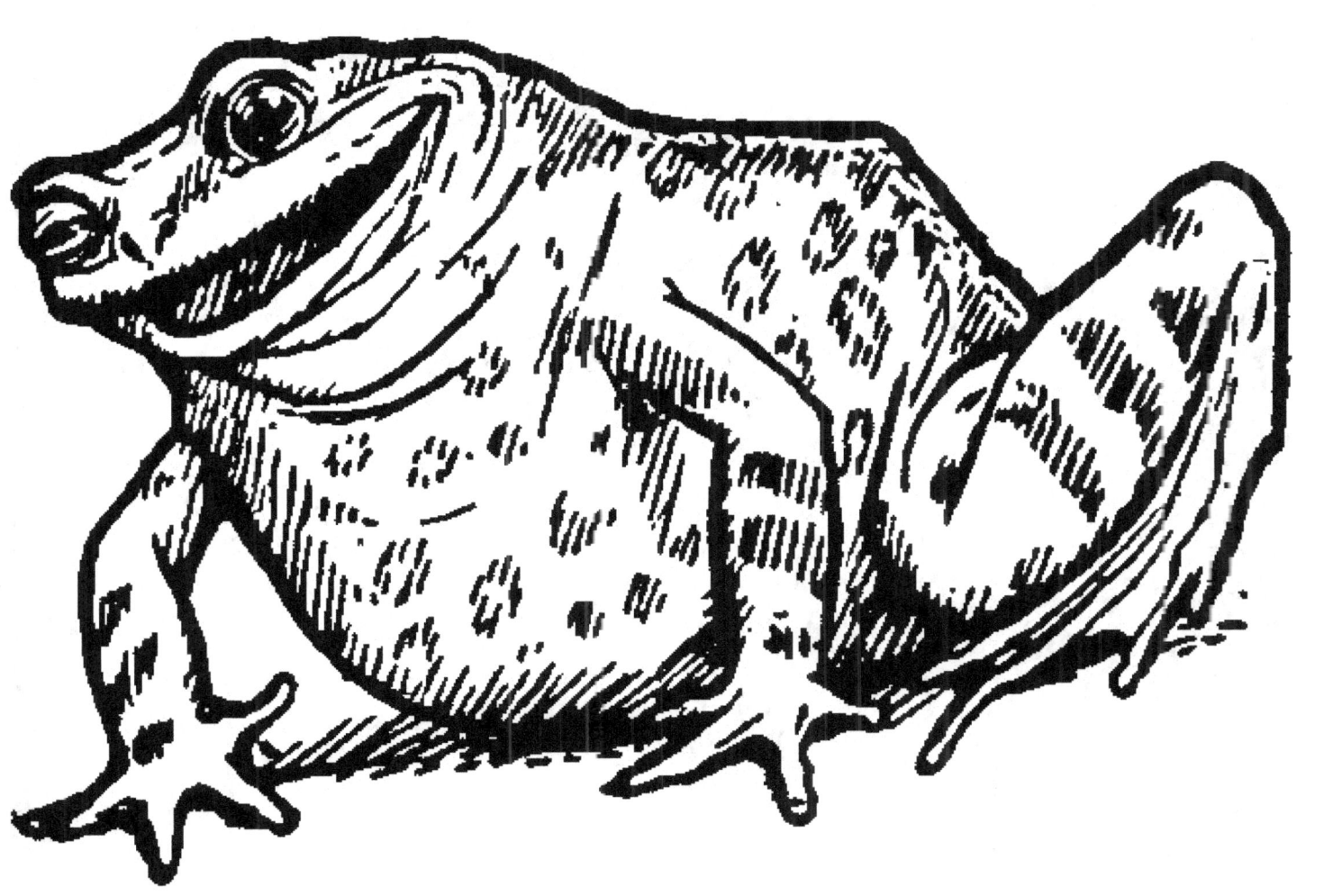

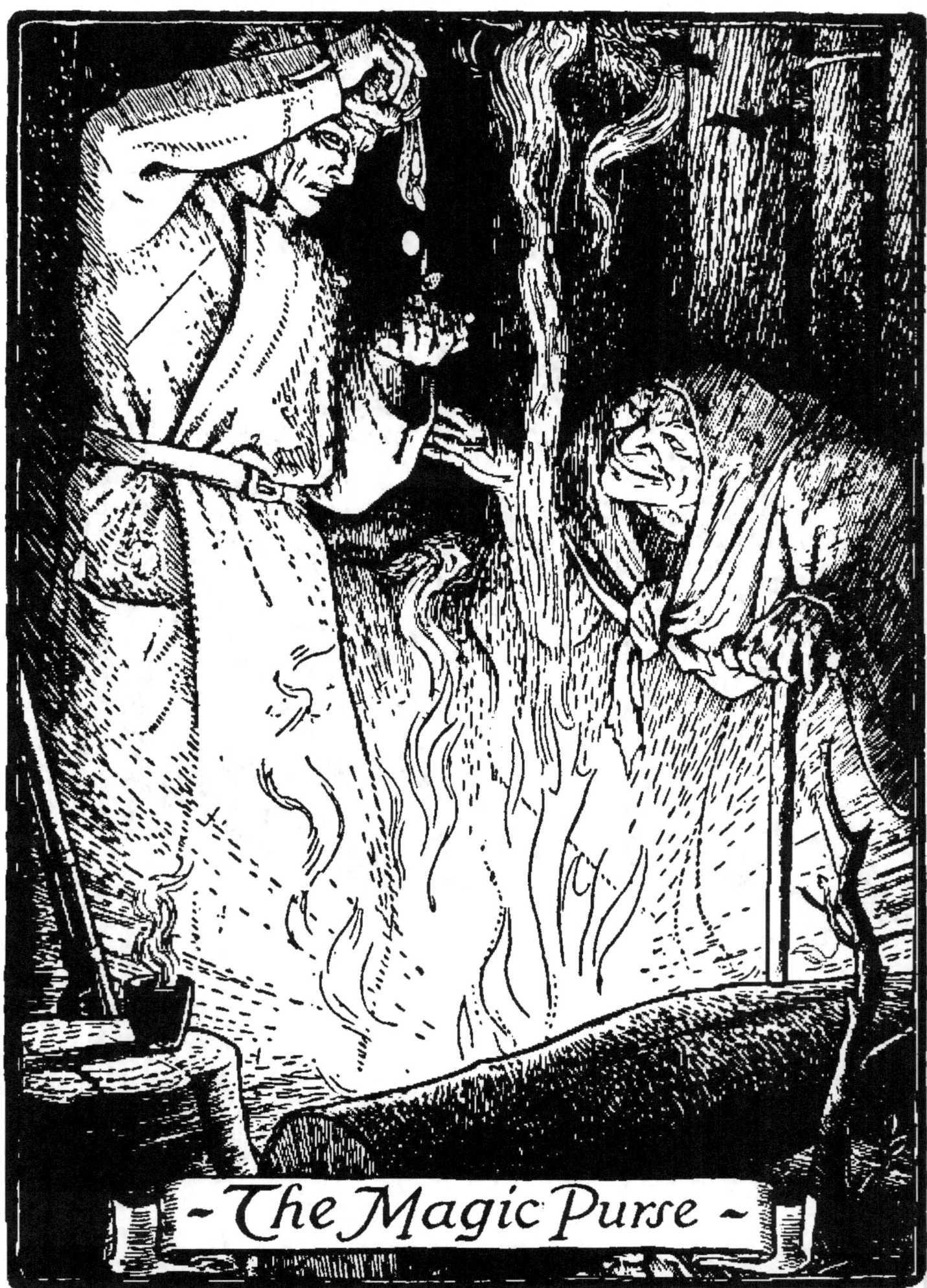

~ The Magic Purse ~

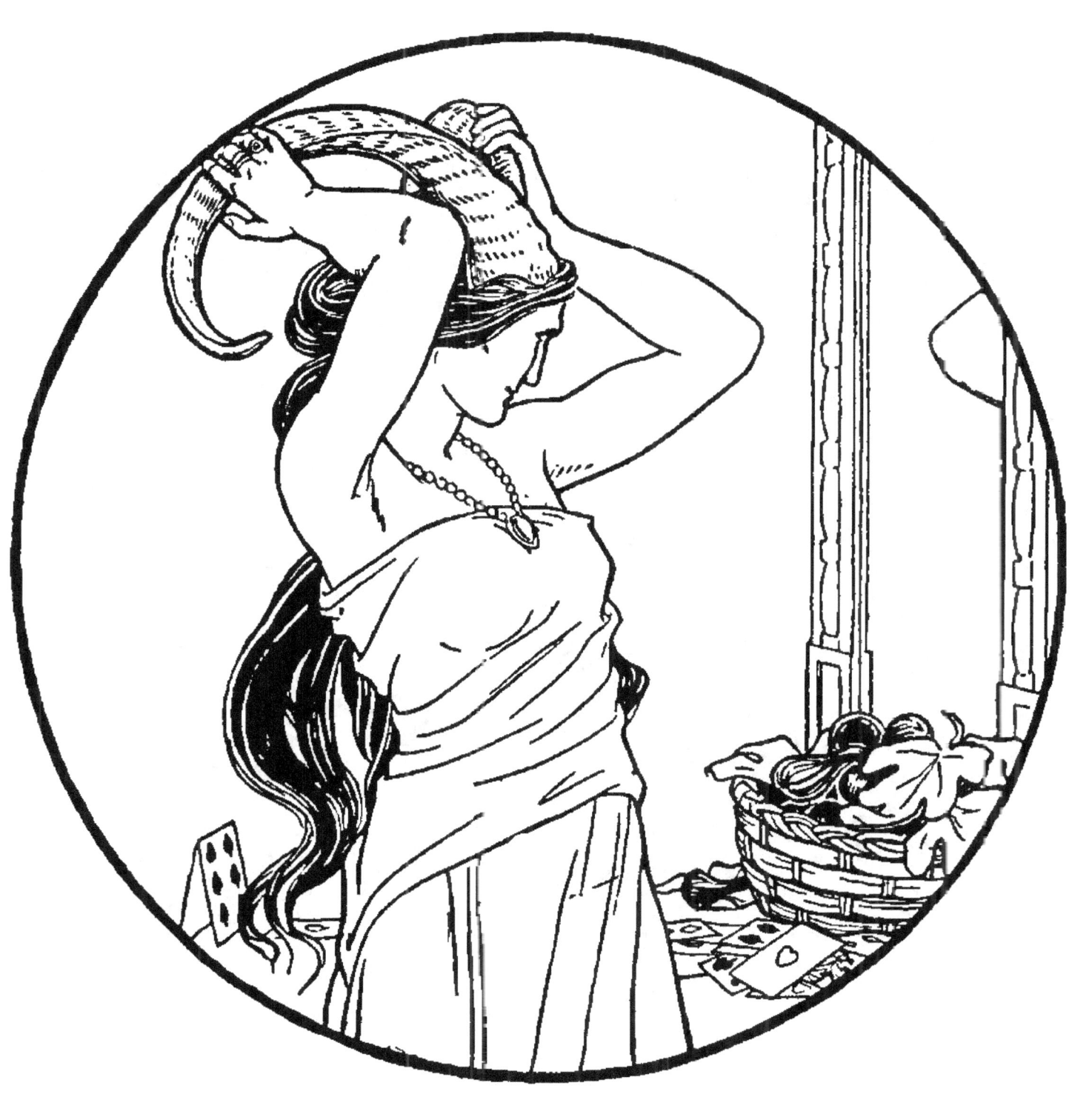

The Princess Finds Horns on her Head

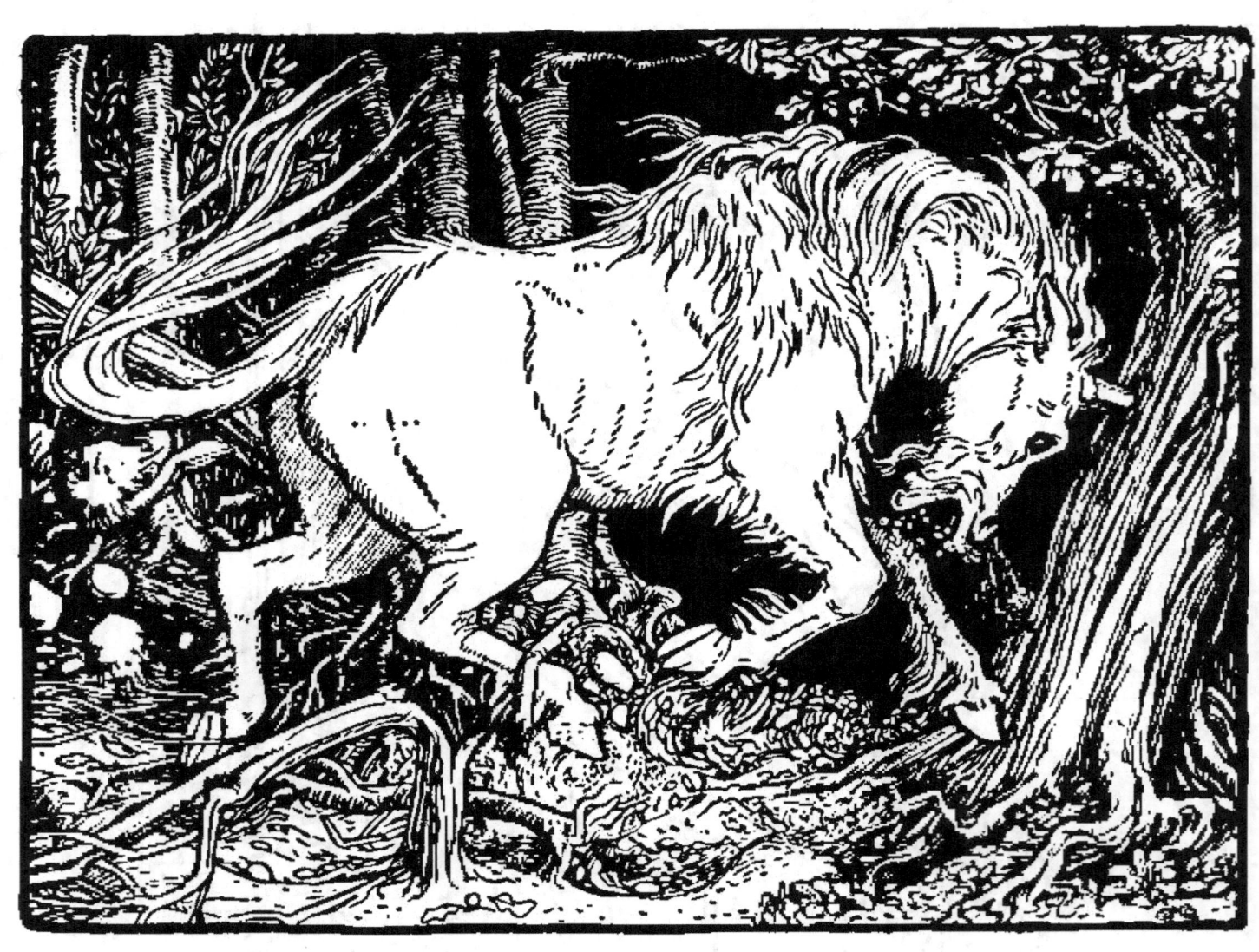

The Unicorn

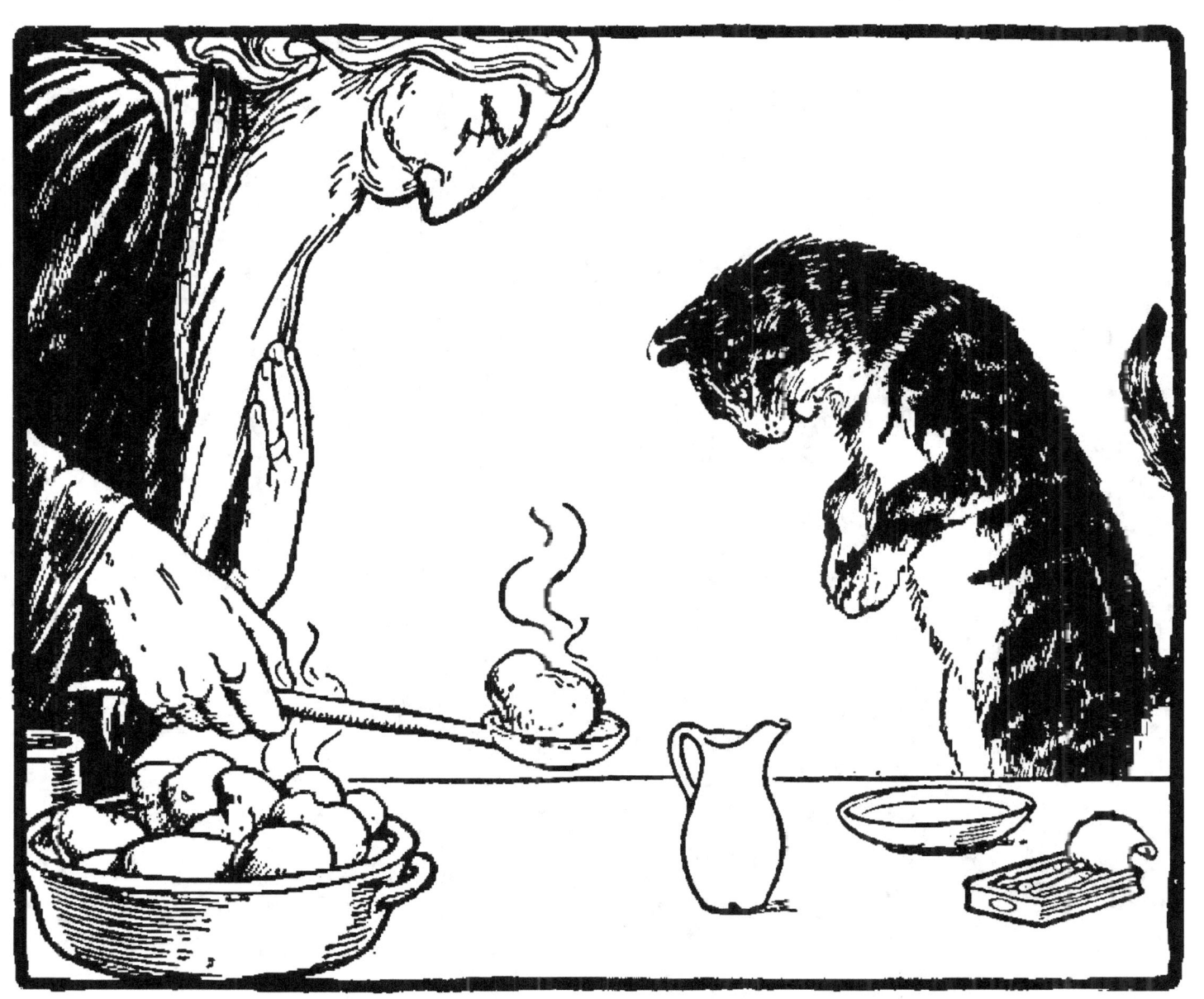

The Earl of Cattenborough will be Pleased to Partake of a Potato

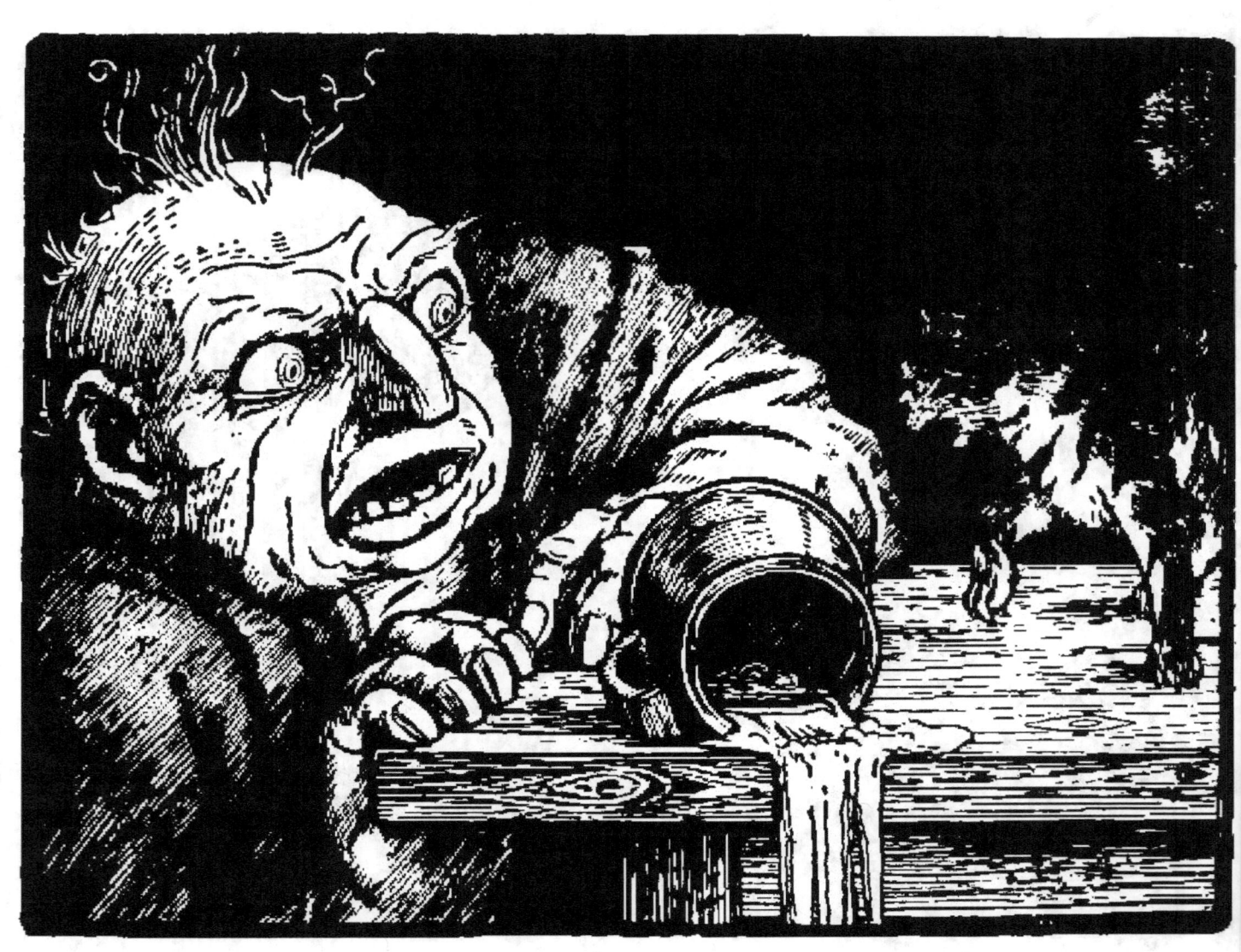

The Cat and the Ogre

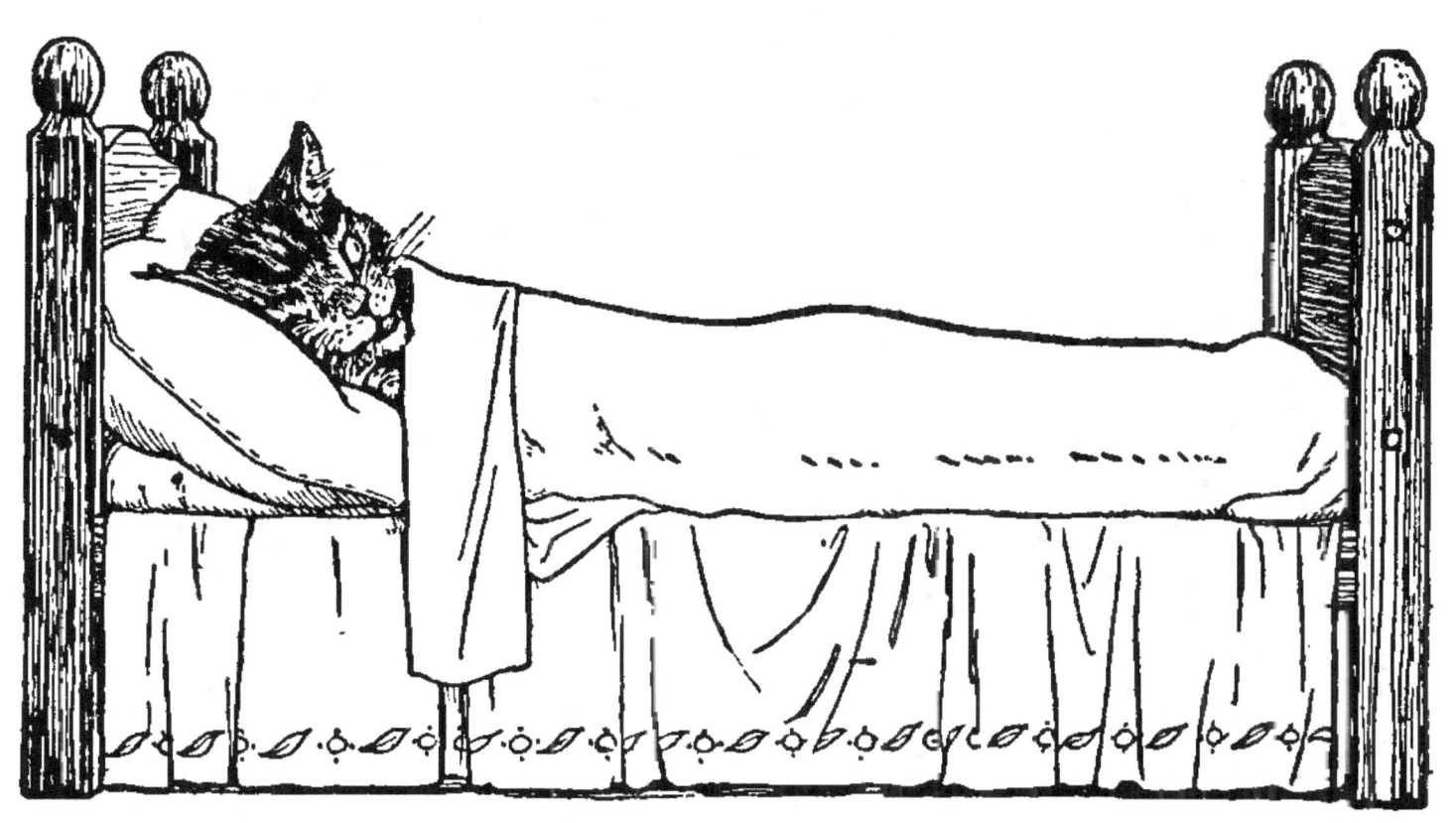

"Had You not Better Throw me into the Millstream?"

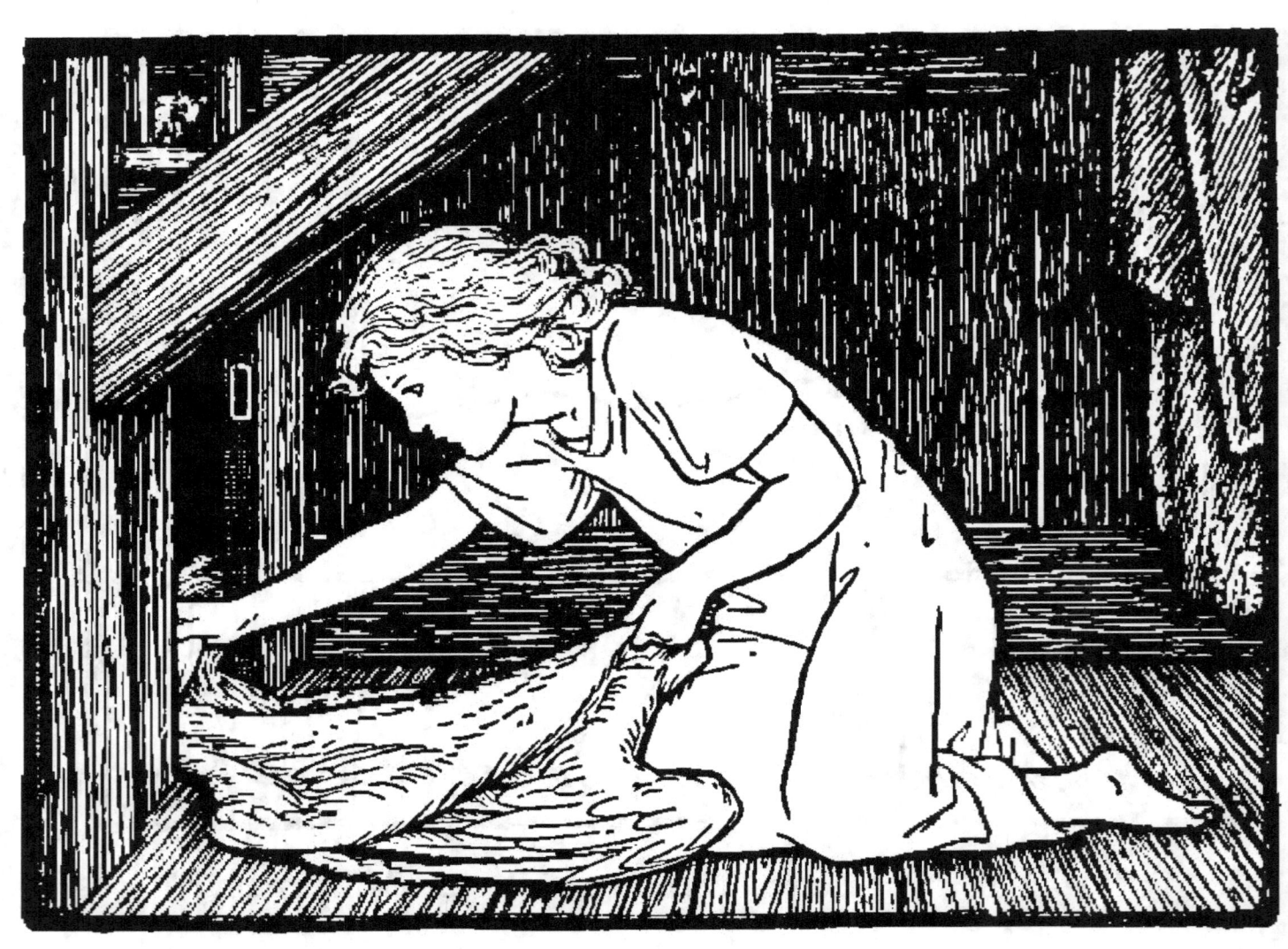

The Child Finds the Feather Dress

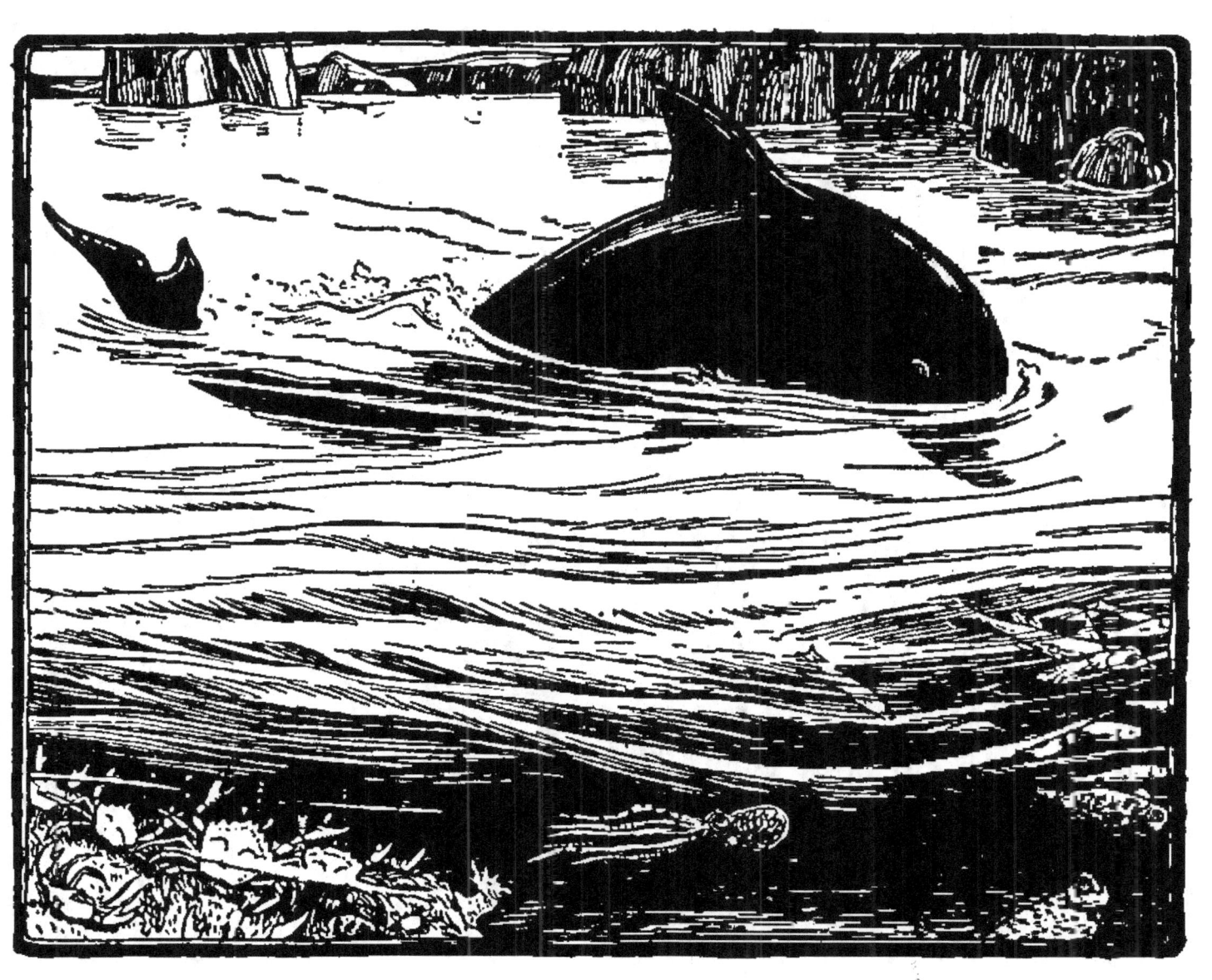

The Dolphin who Came Late

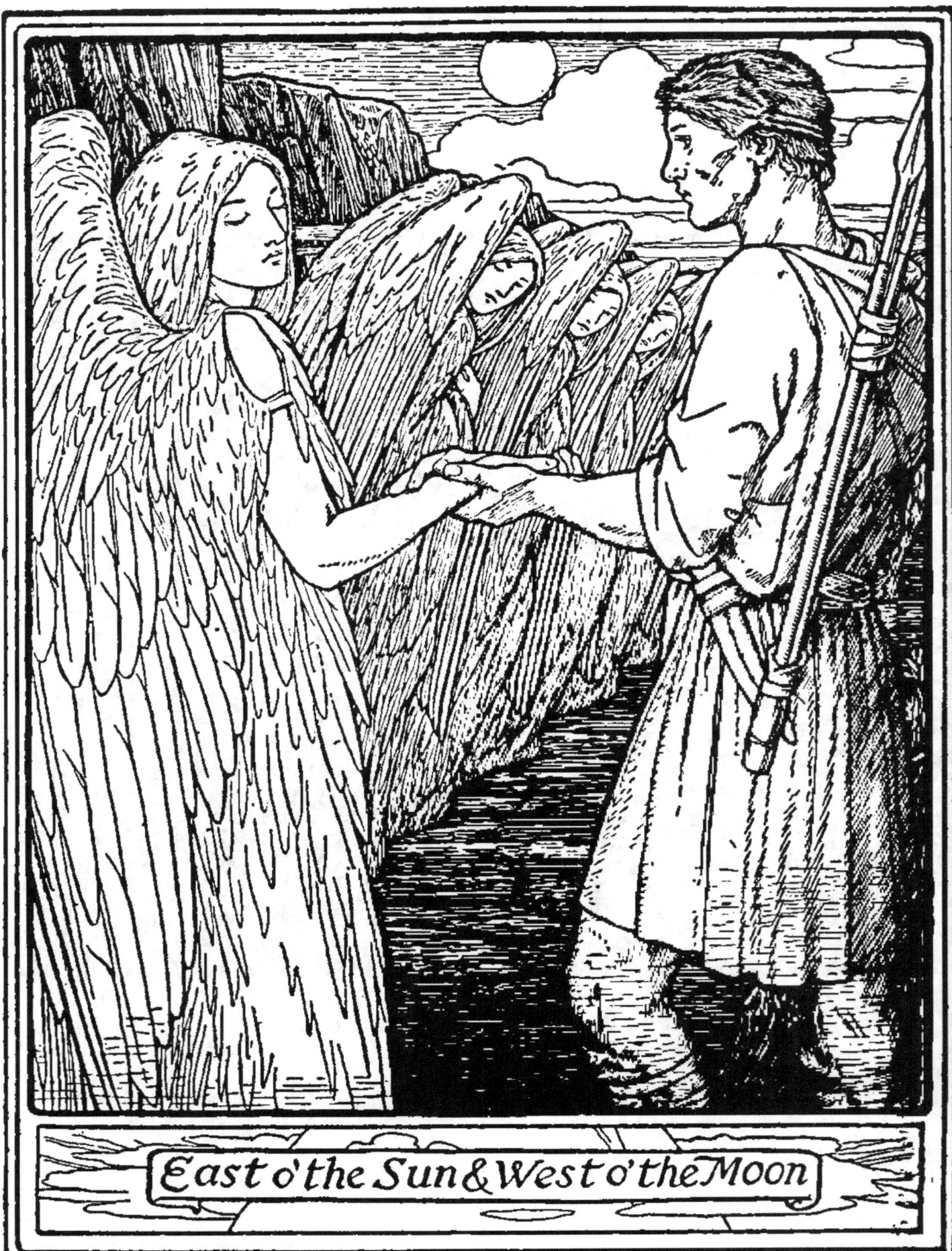

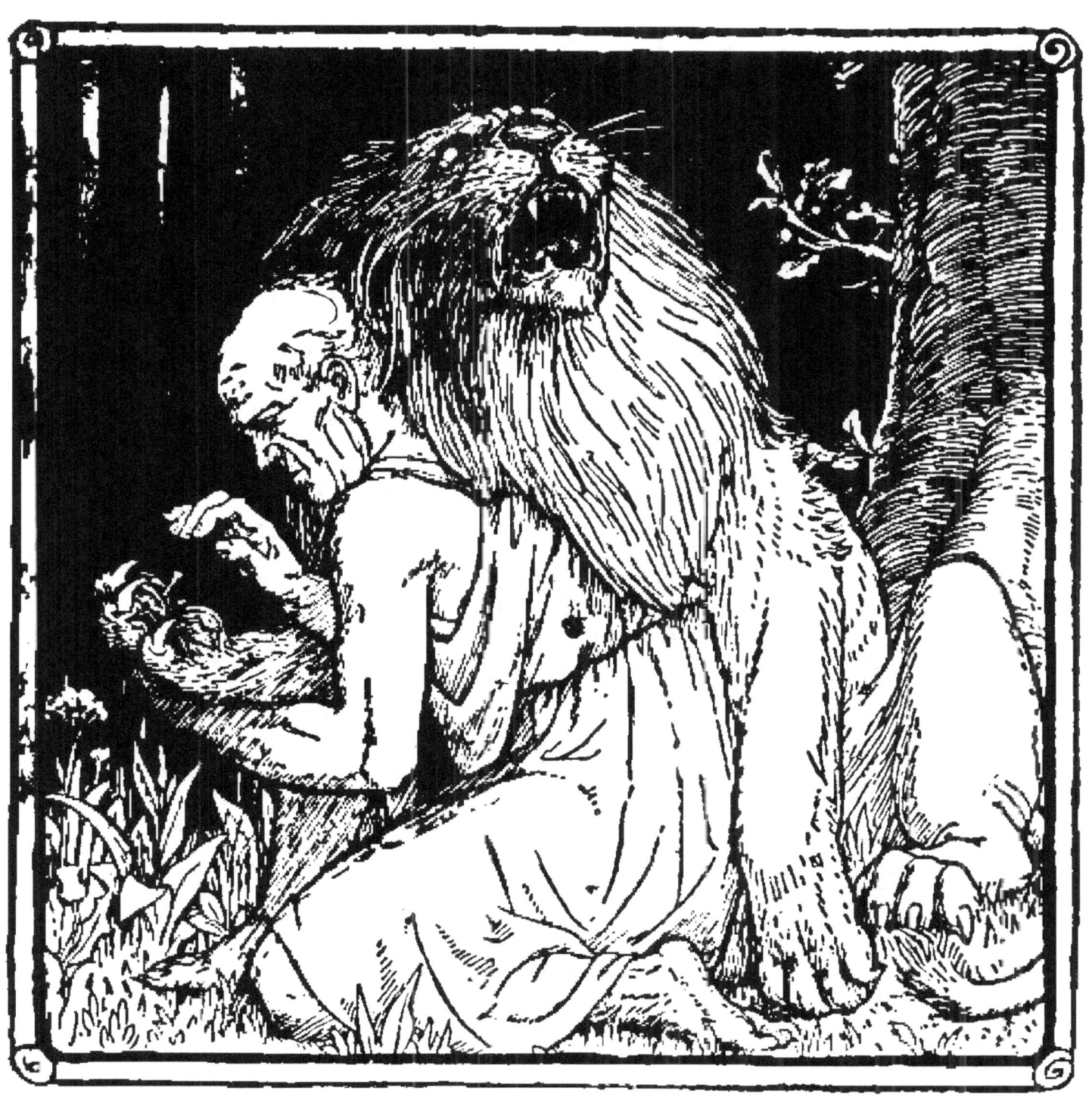

Androcles and the Lion

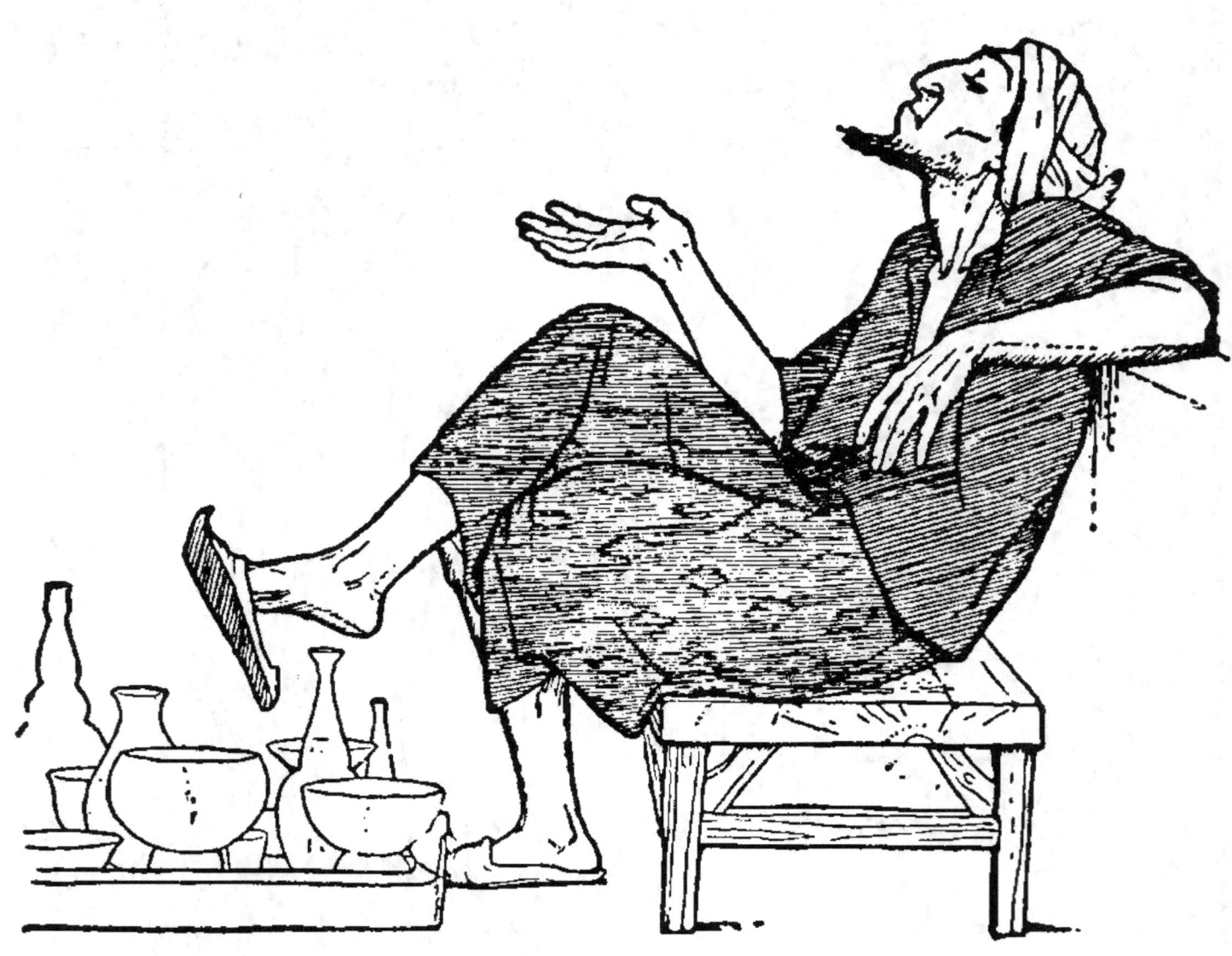

Day-Dreaming

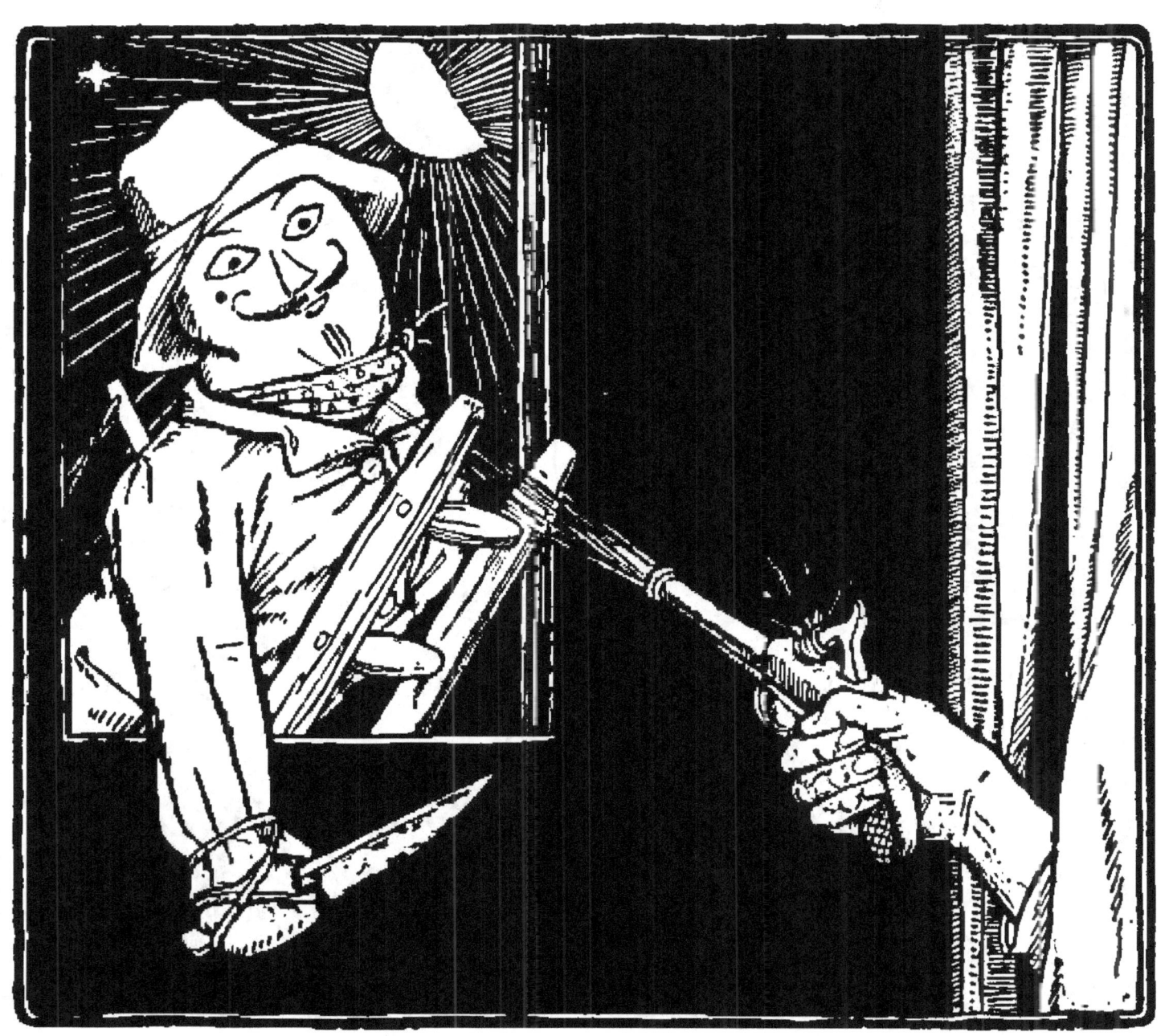
The Dummy

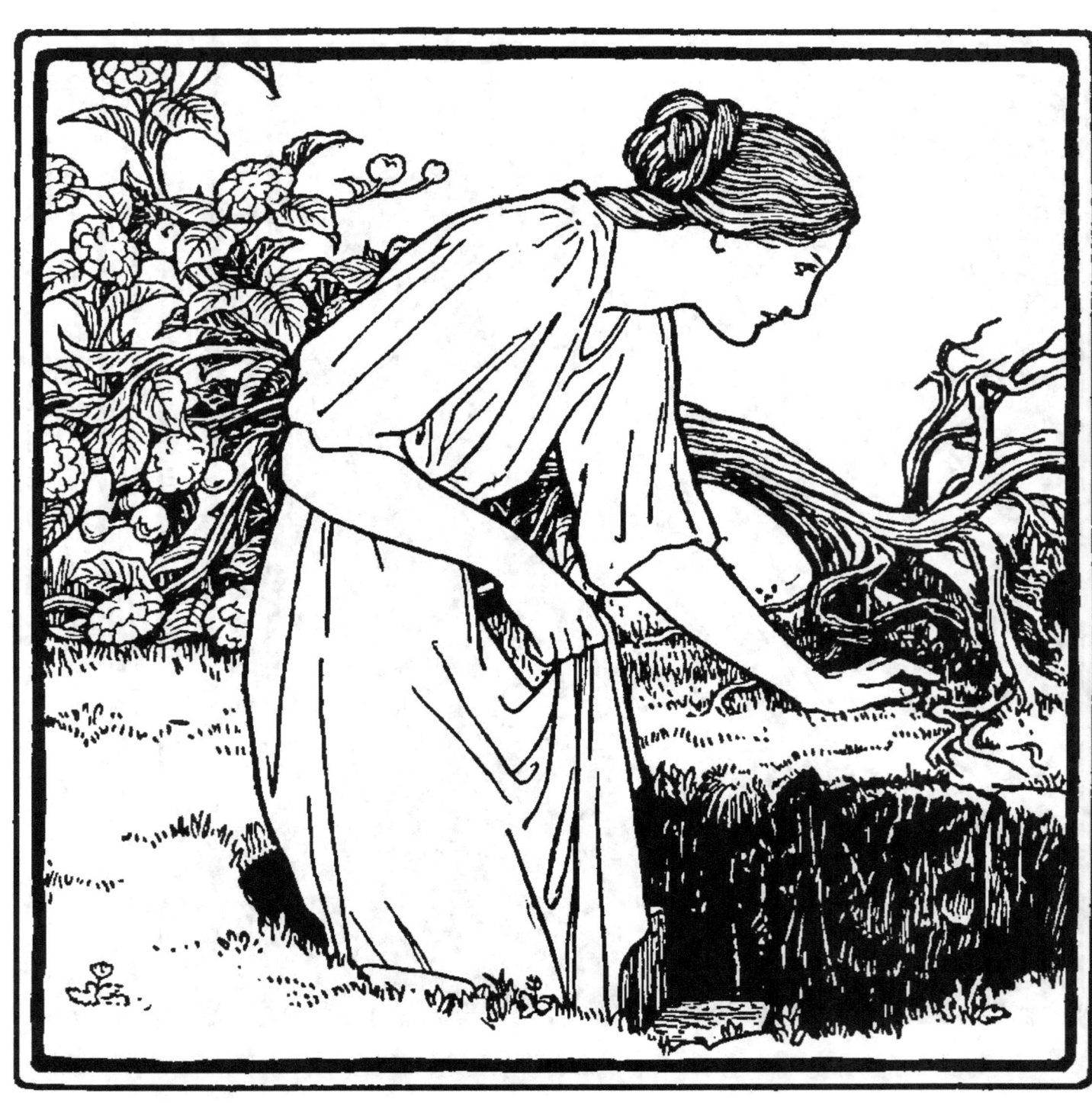

Anima Goes down the Hole

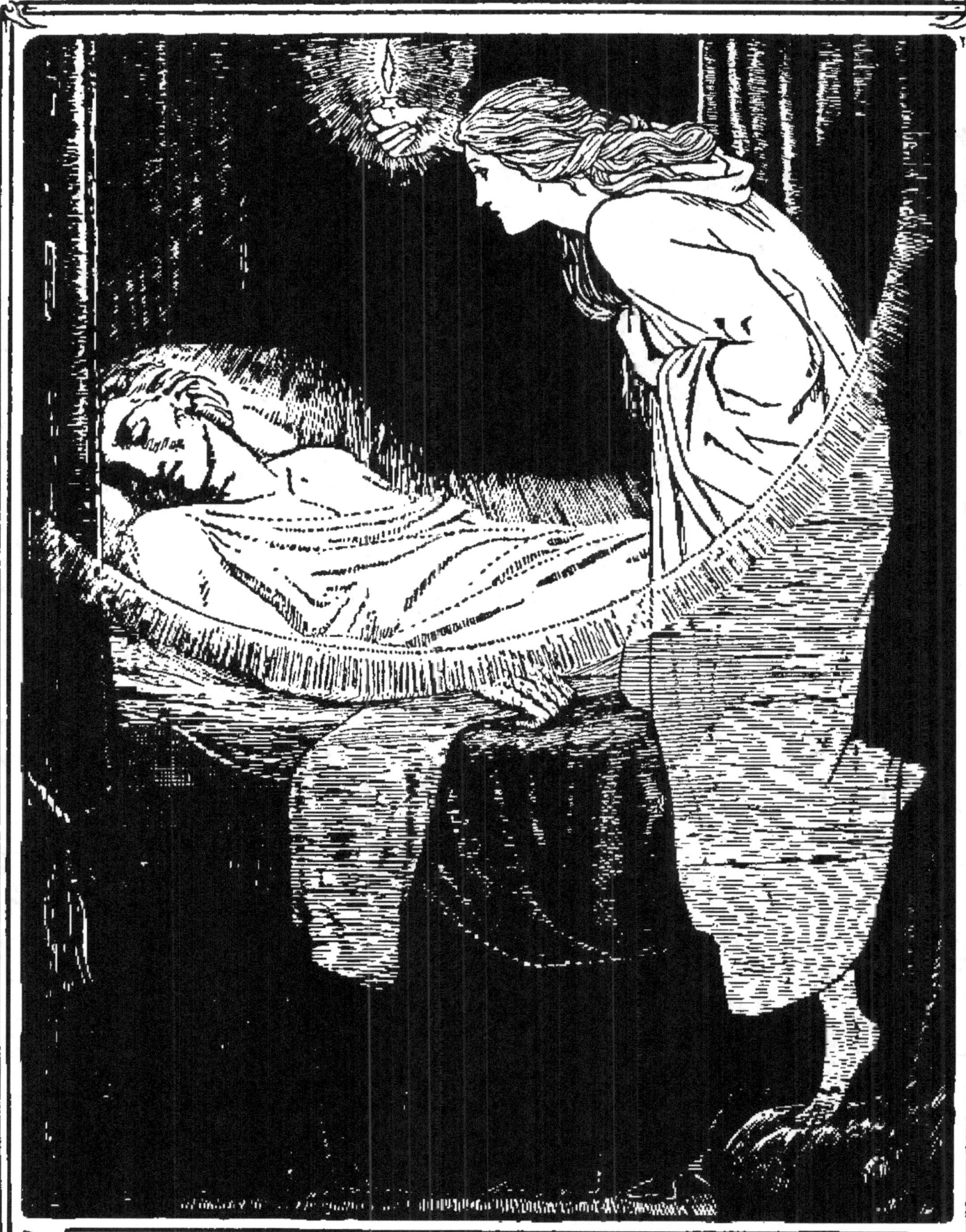

The Lamp

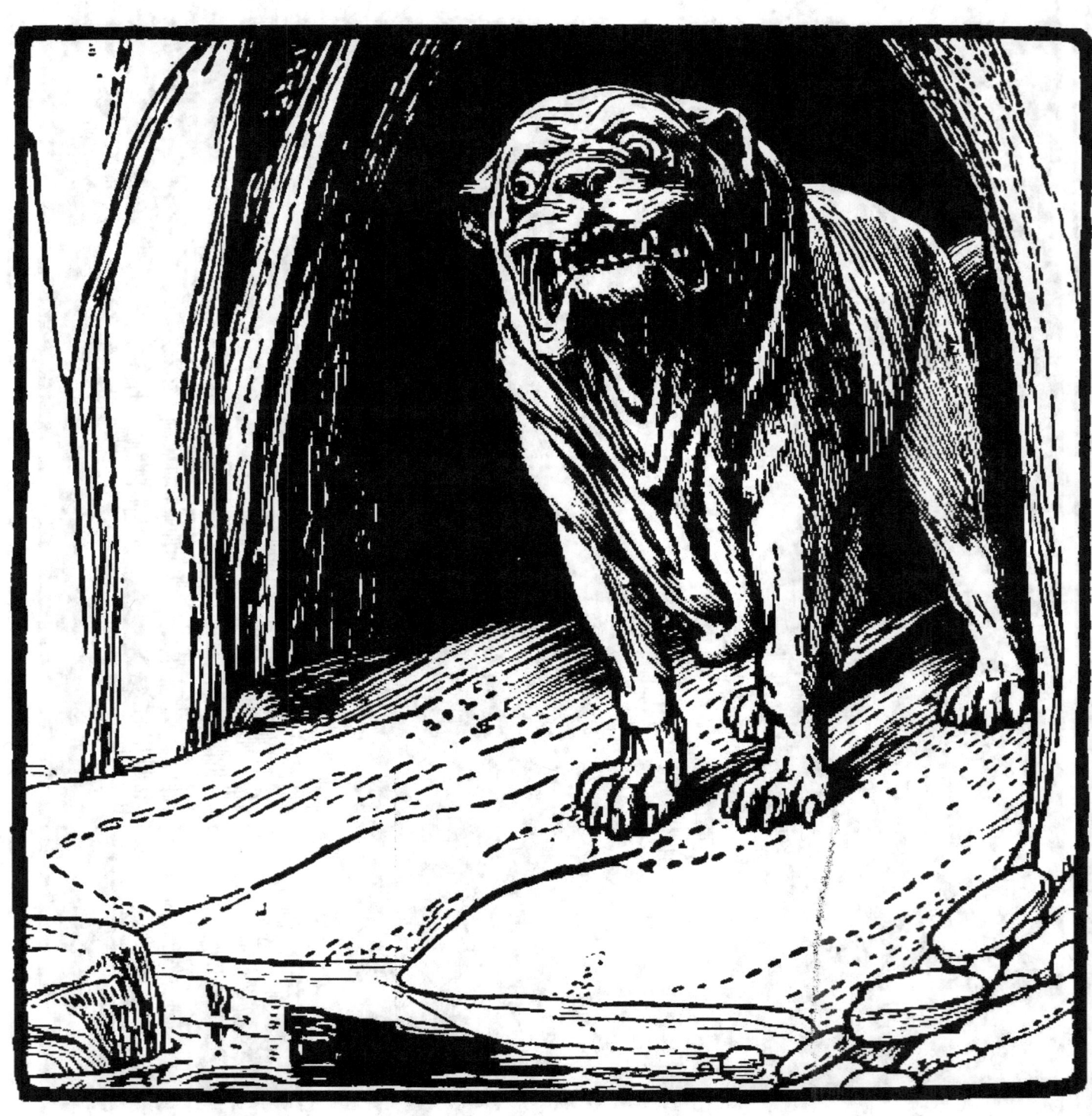

The Dog

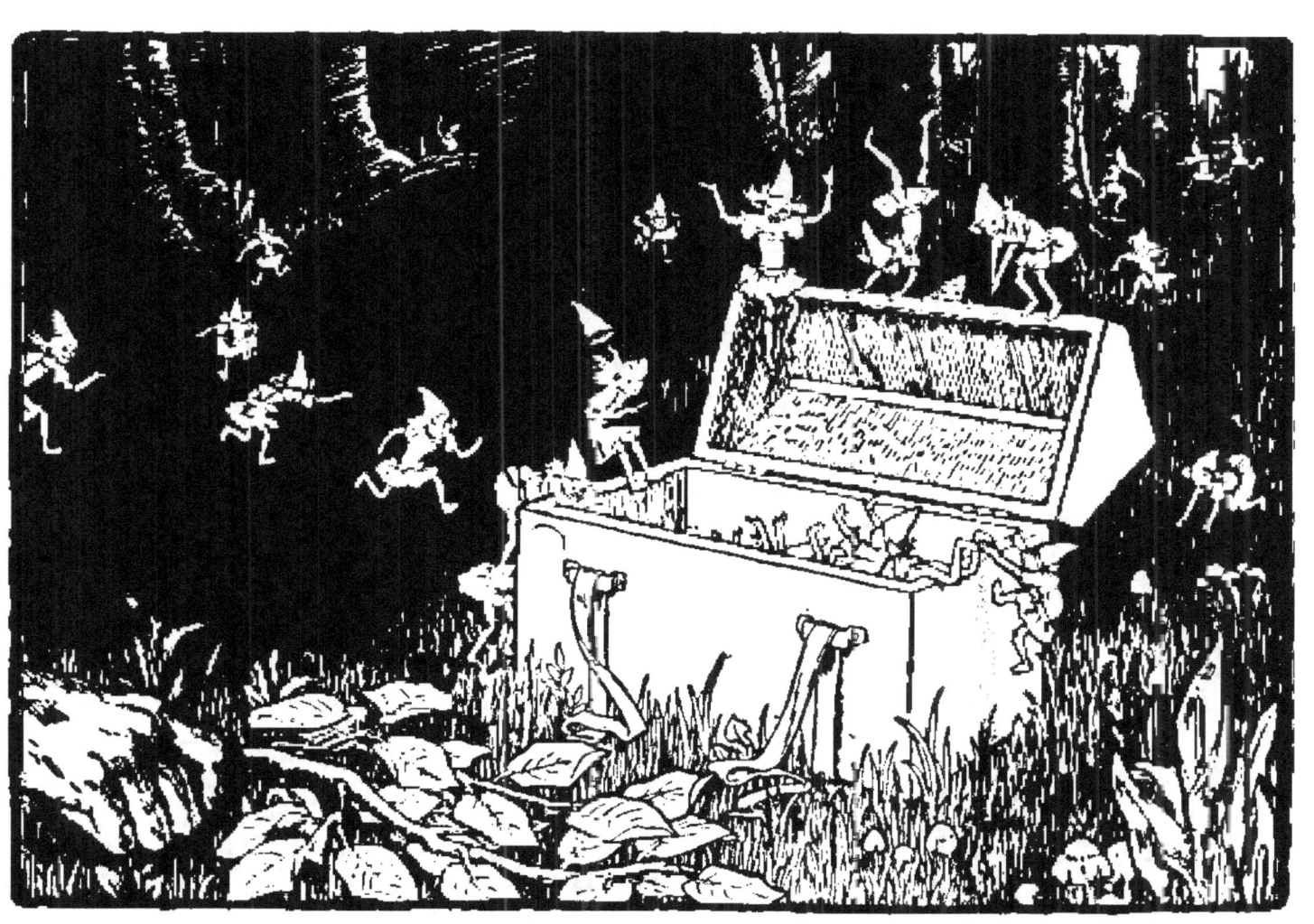

The Casket

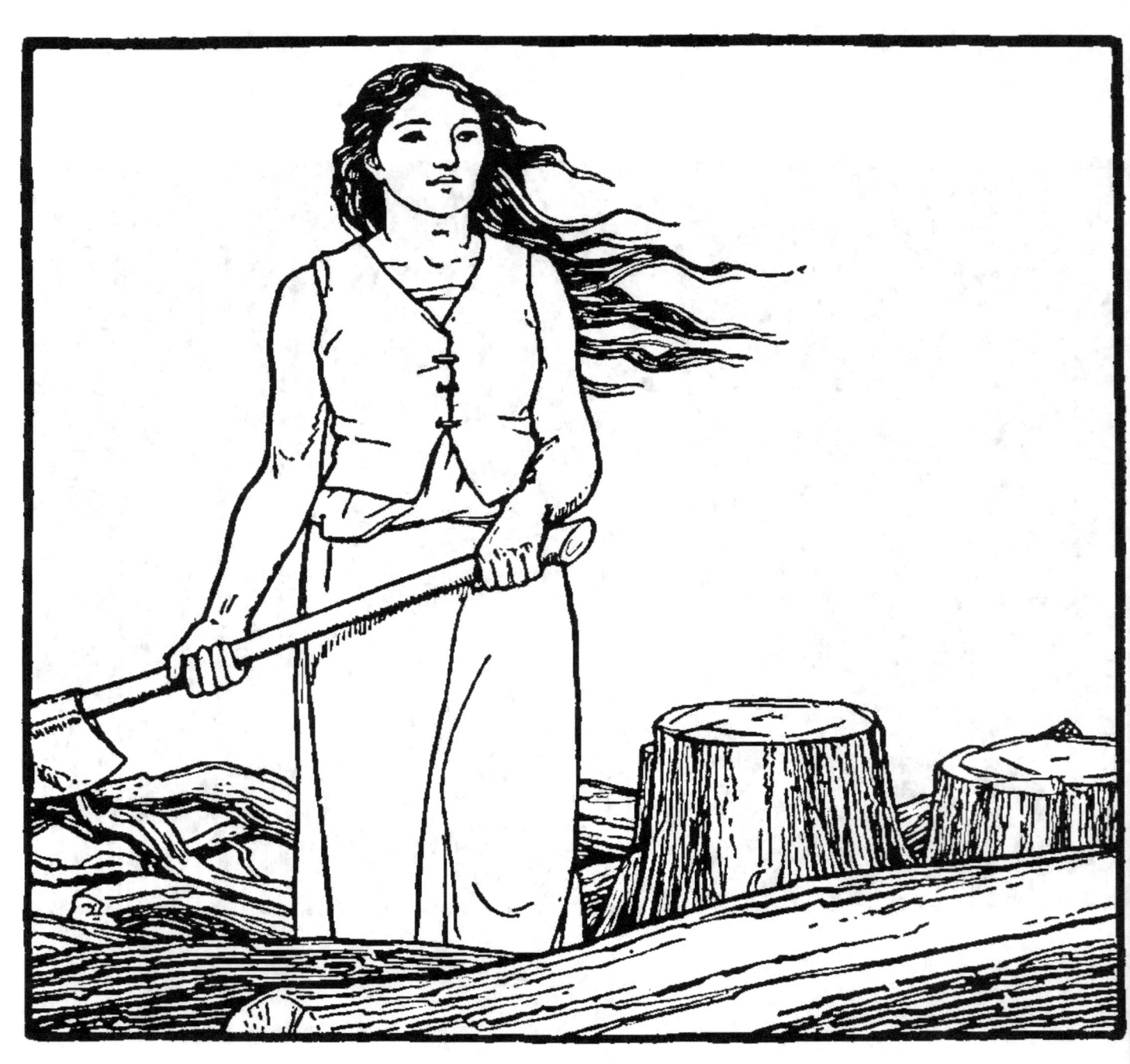

The Master-Maid with the Glass Axe

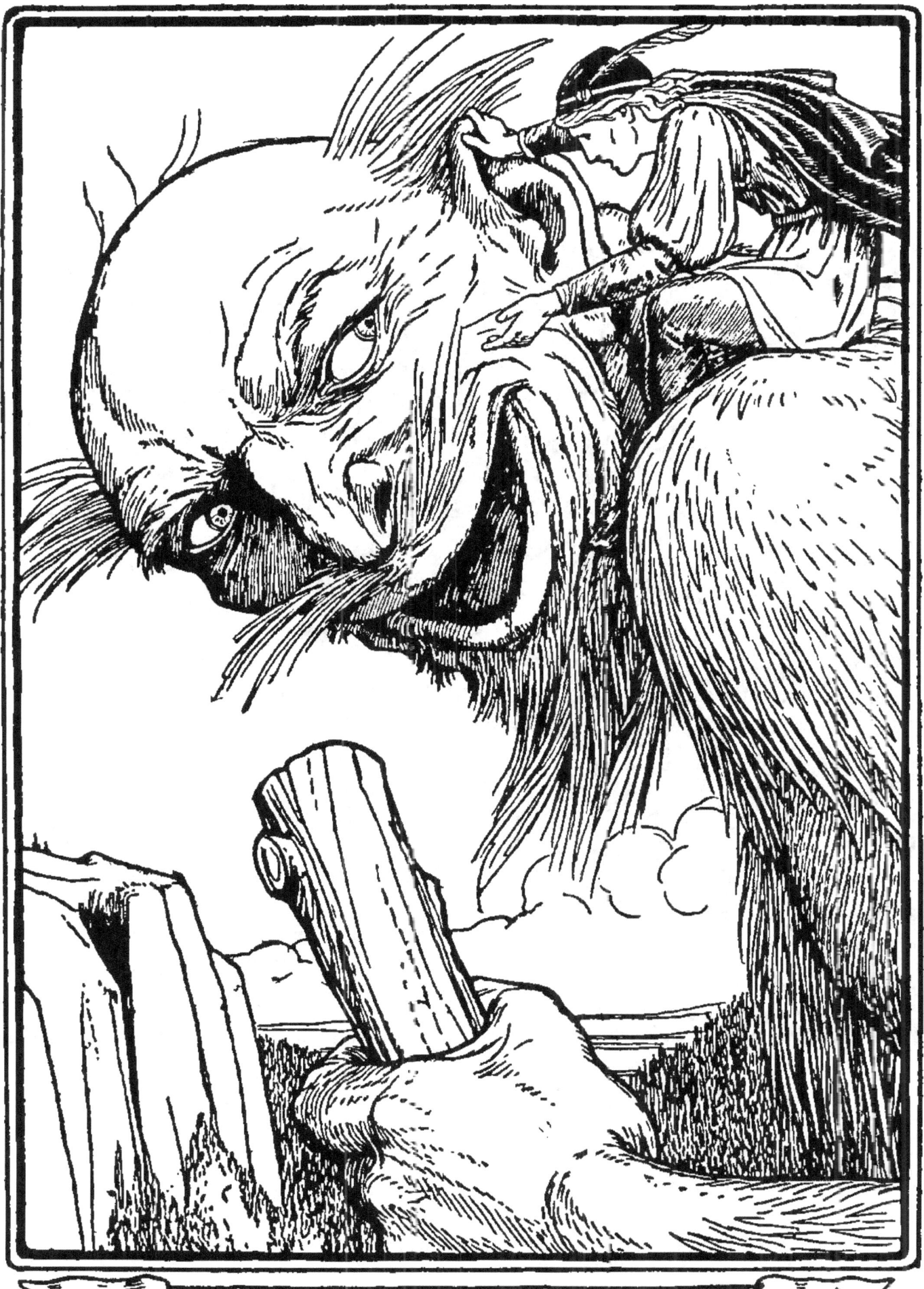
The Prince wants his Lunch

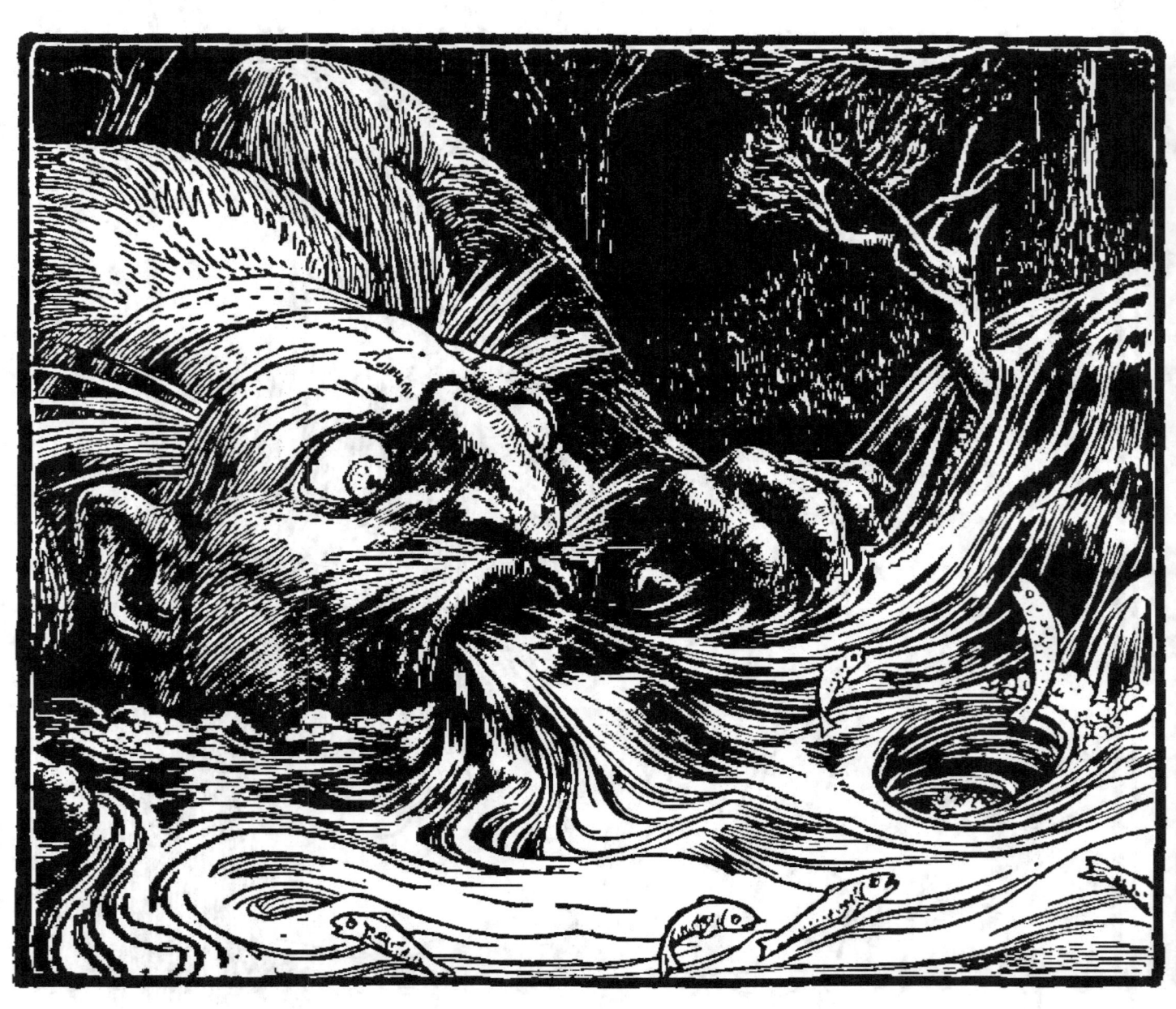

The Giant Tries to Drink the Stream

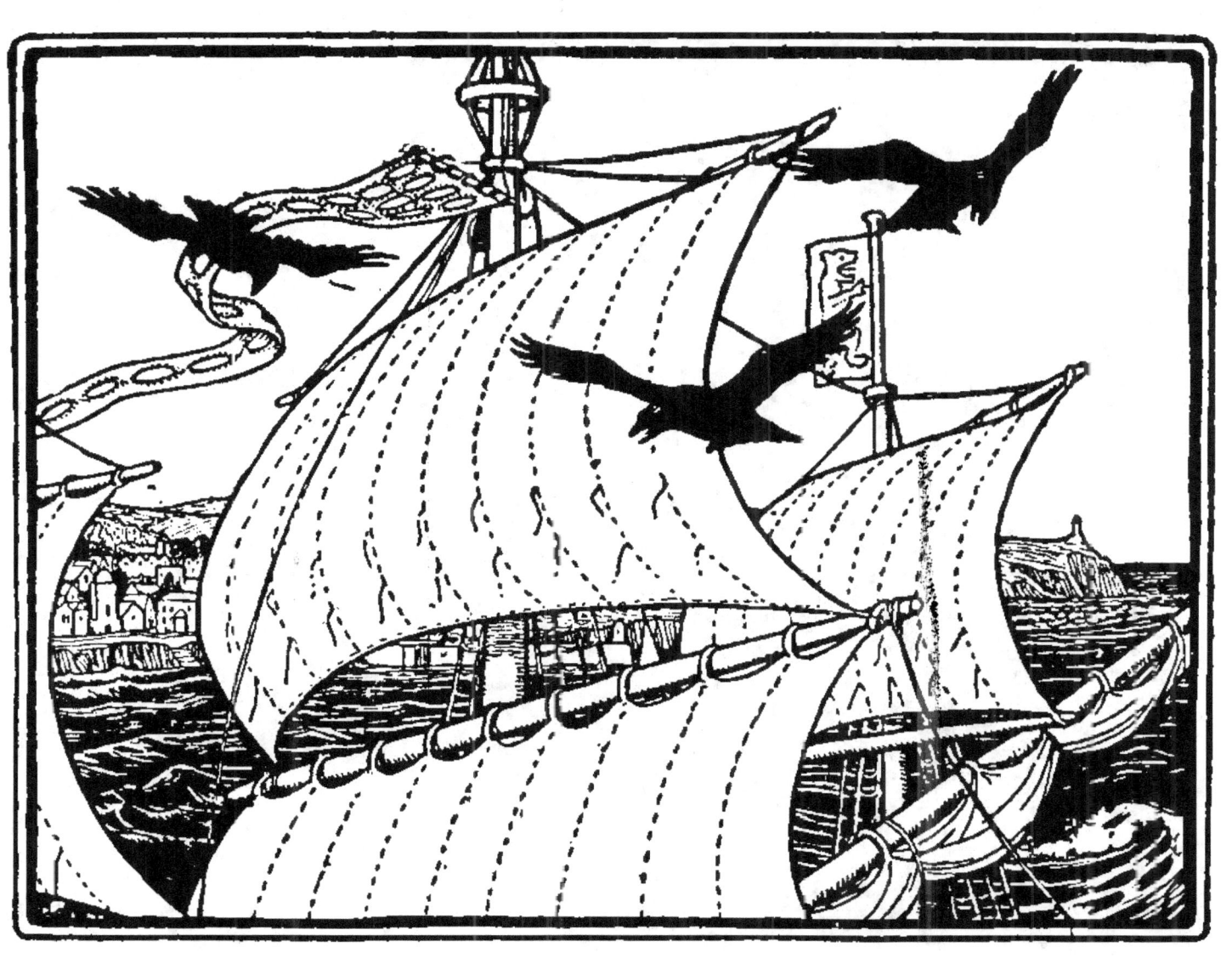

The Three Ravens

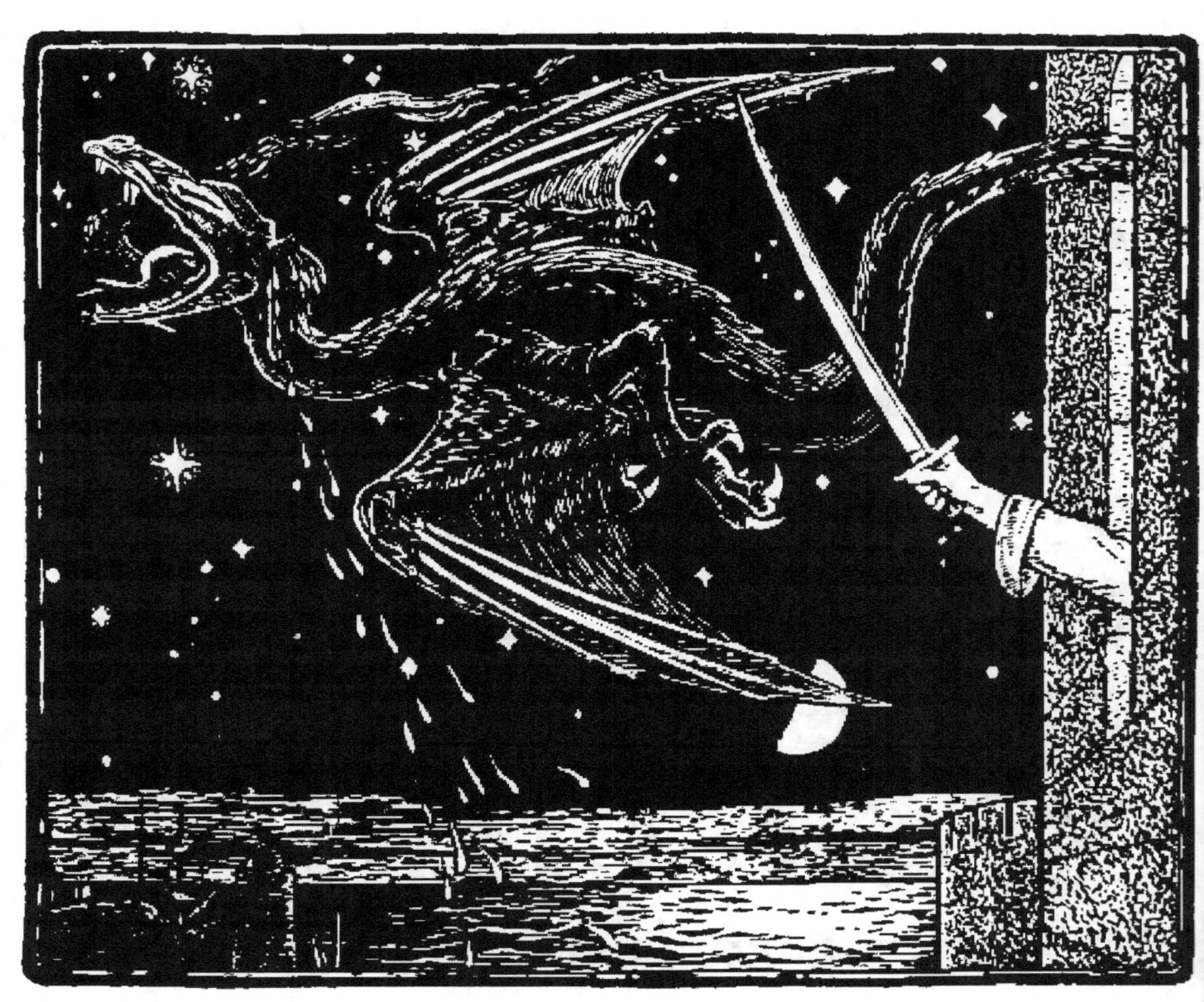

The Wounded Dragon

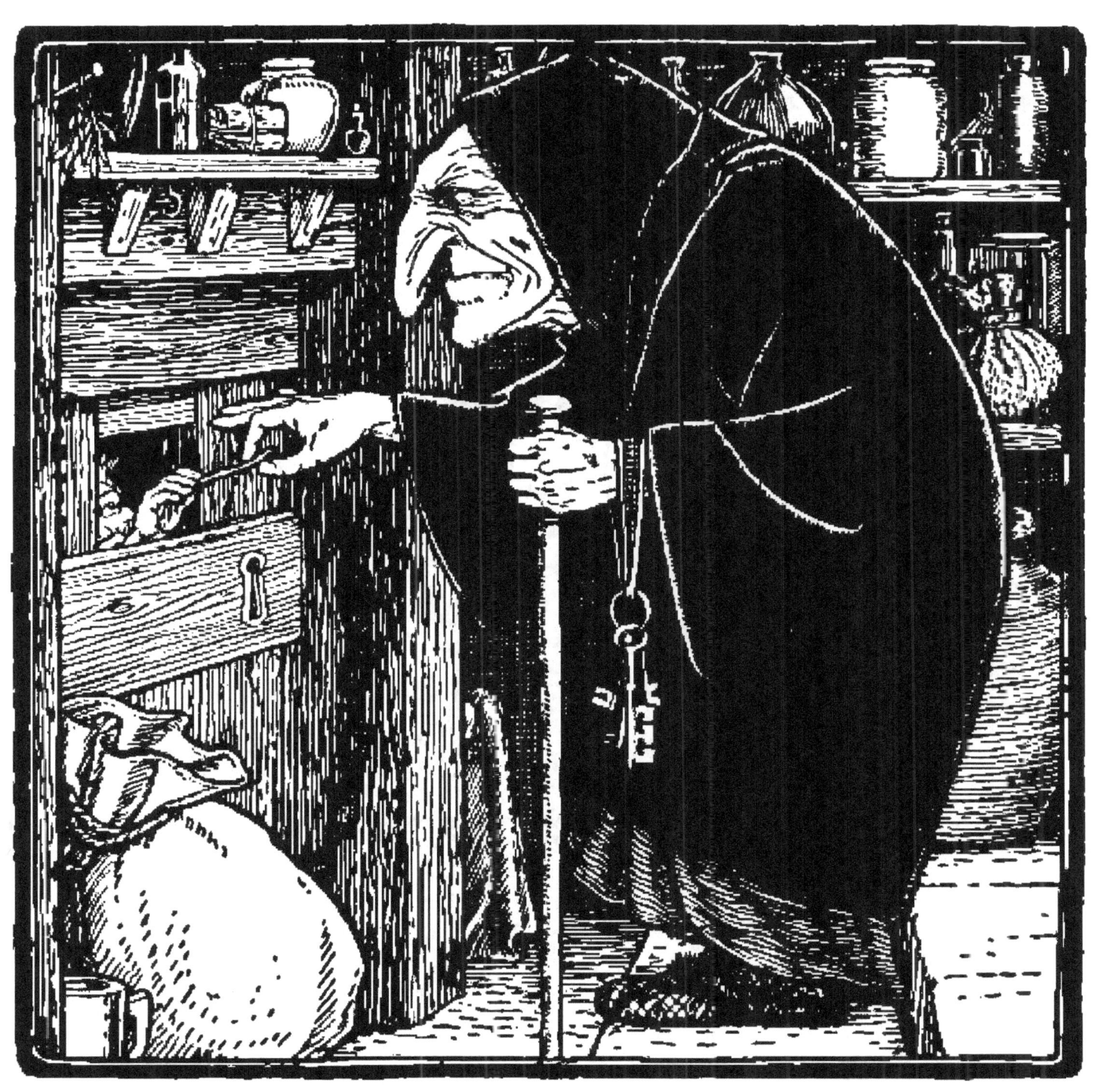

The Witch

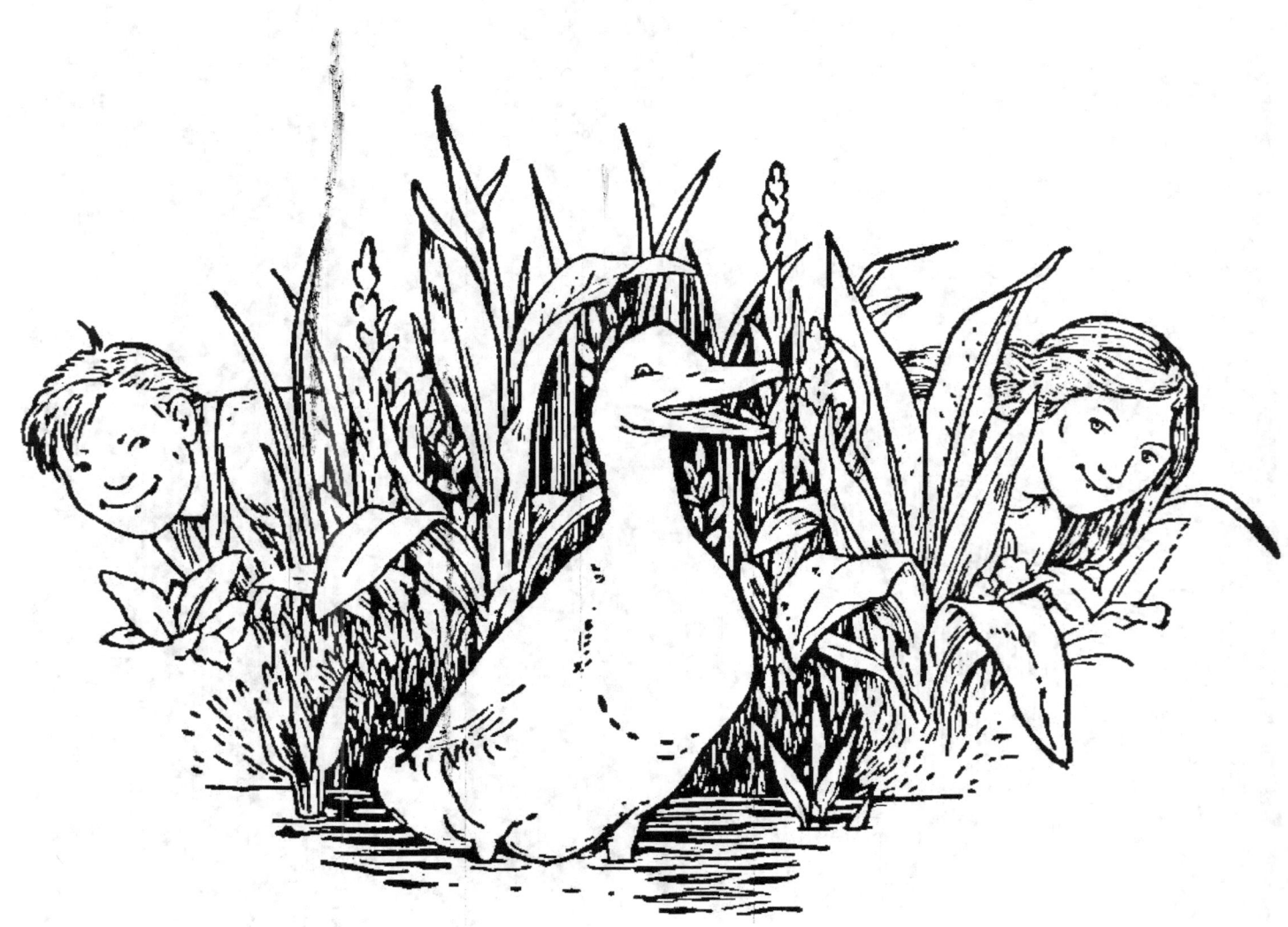

The Duck

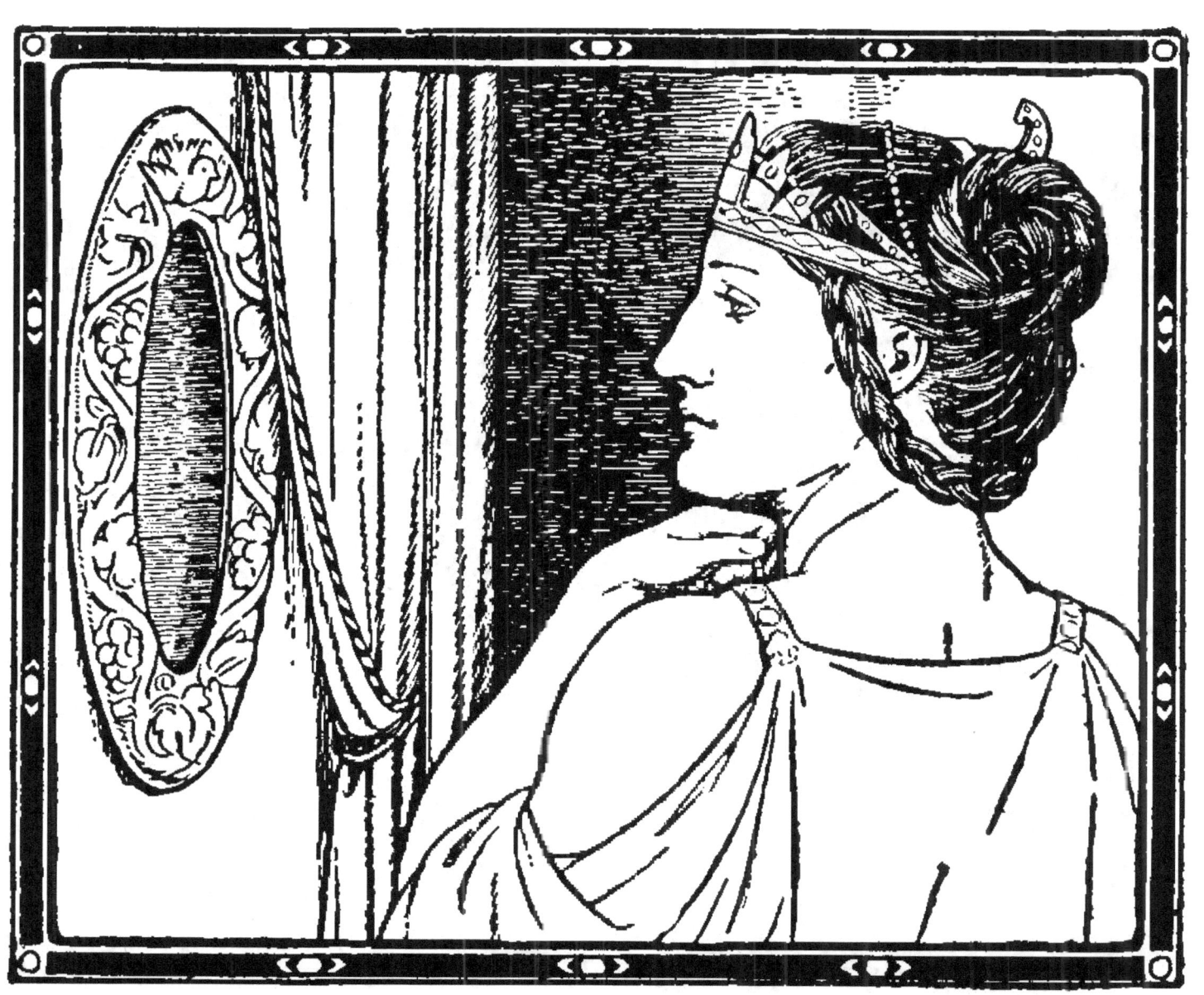

"Mirror, mirror, on the wall,
Who is the fairest of us all?"

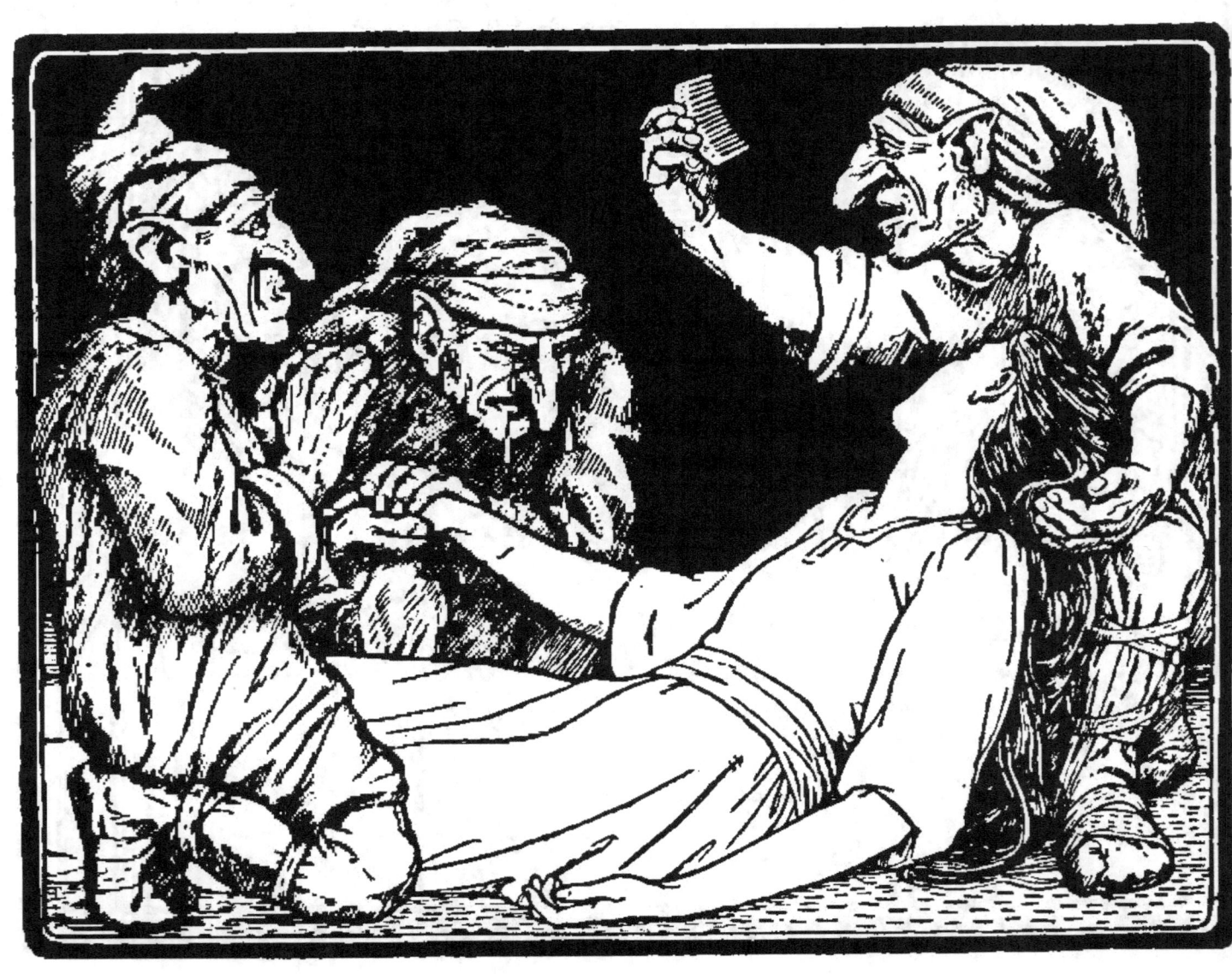

Snowwhite and the Three Dwarfs

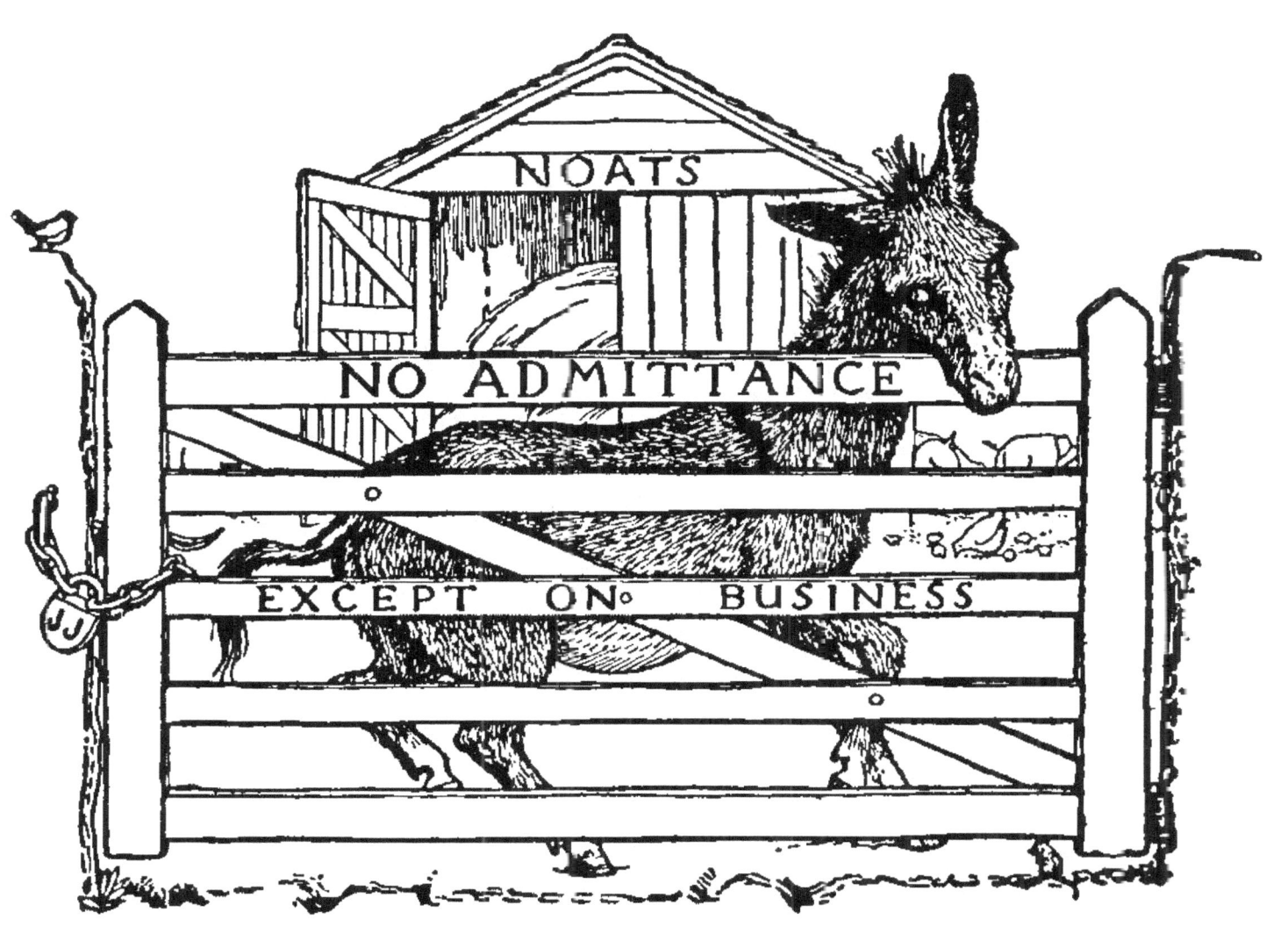

www.ingramcontent.com/pod-product-compliance
Lightning Source LLC
Chambersburg PA
CBHW082124220526
45472CB00009B/2289